THE VERY EDGE
Poems

Featured Authors:	Araceli Esparza
	Huascar Medina
	Anne Whitehouse
Editors:	Polly Alice McCann
	Araceli Esparza
Illustrated by:	Samantha Malay
	Mano Sotelo
Designed by:	Kēvin Callahan

FLYING KETCHUP PRESS ®
KANSAS CITY, MISSOURI

Appreciative acknowledgments to the publications in which the following poems previously appeared: Lugor 1948 by Guinotte Wise first appeared in Grey Sparrow Press 2019. "Up the Wall" by Mary Silwance originally published digitally in *Heartland!*, August 19, 2019. "All My Dead" by Joe Weintraub first published in *the Rockhurst Review* in Spring, 2010.

Flying Ketchup Press ® is a trademarked small press seeking submissions through Submittable.com to discover and develop new and diverse voices in poetry and short story. Our dream is to salvage lost treasure troves of written and illustrated work—to create worlds of wonder and delight; to share stories. Maybe yours.

Find us at www.flyingketchuppress.com

All inquiries should be addressed to:
Flying Ketchup Press
11608 N. Charlotte Street, Kansas City, MO 64115.

Library of Congress Control Number: 2020912733

ISBN-13: 978-1-970151-23-7

Epub ISBN: 978-1-970151-24-4

DEDICATION

For those who are on *the very edge* and simply want what
Pablo Neruda called *unity like the Ocean*; want to speak in their mother
tongue and every language they've ever lived and loved in.
To all the words and worlds in between.

MANO SOTELO

Overcome the World, Savior 6

From the Editors

Araceli Esparza: When did this journey start called "The Very Edge"?

Polly Alice: I put out the call for poets in September of 2018, just a month after we had our soft opening for the press.

Araceli Esparza: So how many poets do we have? Where are they from?

Polly Alice: These poems were sent from poets the world over, from the top the Swiss Alps, to the U.S. border, and the sky rises of Manhattan and Tokyo. We have 37 poets and artists in this collection if you include the both of us.

Araceli Esparza: That is impressive!

Polly Alice: So what do you think of them a whole? What do you feel readers will appreciate about this collection?

Araceli Esparza: It's a page turner. I highly recommend that readers go through this collection in short spunks of moments that are bookended with the beautiful photography."

Polly Alice: Yes I like what you said earlier about the poems being powerful. It's like they were written in the back of a truck or in a tent at night. They feel urgent, important. I'm glad you like the art. The art and photography just sort of happened. Poets are artists and artists are poets. However we have two featured artists for this collection. Samantha Malay is the textile designer and photographer poet who is featured on the cover. And Mano Sotelo is the award winning feature artist who I felt captured the perfect visual aspect of this book with his meditative portraits that capture someone living at an intersection that I would call "the very edge." I have to mention Janet McMillan Rives and Omar Bárcena who sent vibrant photography.

Araceli Esparza: Yes, the art is important in this book. It takes me on a journey. I think these images reflect the poems so that you are allowing a new light to come into the narrative. And who are the poets featured in this collection?

Polly Alice: "This collection features three main poets, but there are forty additional poets in all. Poet Laureate of Kansas, Huascar Medina graciously sent us three poems to feature. The one called *The New Americans*, I heard him perform it in person and I've kept hearing it in my mind ever since, especially as I worked on this book. Anne Whitehouse who is a prolific New York poet, journalist and book reviewer. And you are the third featured poet, Araceli. I love the way your poems helped root the others. They get to the quick center of personal emotions behind how political actions can affect our daily breath, our daily identity, and our daily choice of word--and even more so of the poet. I wanted the collection to serve first as a table for international poets to gather around with our words to cross borders.

Araceli Esparza: What is the heart of the book?

Polly Alice: I've gathered these voices to show how much we are all the same, how we all face borders and boundaries of the mind, the heart, the spirit, and of course, political borders which threaten to divide us. What would you tell writers? How can we support each other at this time?

Araceli Esparza: I'd say the message is already in this book: to be a welcome beam of light—to be a reflection of acceptance. We all believe in the power of belonging. The traditions of social justice have shifted, and we need to stay nimble for these new waves. In this book we read and see that narrative. Last Words?

Polly Alice: I think we should thank these poets and artists for their gentle fierceness for putting our borders and boundaries into words, so we can carry them with us and continue to push for a multicultural literary community. We are deeply grateful for the featured visual artists.

Araceli Esparza: And a reminder that while we strive to present all languages with dignity and respect, we let the dialect of different poets and their regions speak for themselves. Over grammatically correct language, we focused on the emotional tinder. When it came to choosing correct "Spanish" we chose poetic license and the poets everyday way of speaking. Our focus was to represent a visual and authentic voice.

Polly Alice: Yes, to create an array of natural, lyrical voices to bring our edges together. To mend.

Both: We hope you enjoy the multitude of voices and journeys in this book.

Table of Contents

BIRD

MOUNTAIN

NIGHT

KEY

Poems are like Salsa. "Kick up your wordplay temperature gauge all the way to 100!"

Enjoy the "curiosity of language" Bring those words up to a curiosity level from a 1 to a 10.

Use fragments. Or use ornamentation. (Get a little crazy.) Try a paradox. Take big leaps.

Give yourself more freedom. Keep your poems warm the way artists look at their art. They walk by and they walk by again. So read your poem all week to keep it warm. Don't revise it. Just enjoy it. Maybe tweak here or there---and on the weekend you are ready to finish your poem. It's kept warm for you.

Write a poem in any language you want. Switch back and forth. Pick one to start in, one to finish it, and in the middle do confetti style!

"Light the fuse!"

Remember. "You are virtuosos, and you have many instruments."

Sutured

sutured gaping eyes sutured gaping eyes sutured gaping eyes sutured gaping eyes sutured gaping eyes sutu

watch me etch respite into my
arteries with a black tar bayonet
watch me   watch me pontificate
watch me pull potion watch me
vomit it back out watch me break
        shit watch   me watch me
                        punctuate the
walls with my own blood cells
        watch me watch you do it too
        watch

(surrounding field composed of the repeated word "watch", with the diagonal edge repeating "sutured gaping eyes sutured gaping eyes sutured gap")

como el yermo

les terres désolées

like a desert

POLLY ALICE MCCANN

Santo-frais

ARACELI ESPARZA

Rotten Apples

My apples come from cactuses 500 years old
  I have big dreams for this little lady called liberty
  But she ain't meet my mother tho
  She clean like a virgin
  We call her Guadalupe
  She makes pennies into dollars
  Sends them right back from where they call her
  You thought what you knew, but you didn't know
  what you did know
  and she came back and told
  me *sit tight honey*
  because our time is now,
  our time is now,
  your time is now,
  our time is now.

HUASCAR MEDINA

Same Ol' News—for Pedro Pietri

We still work

Sometimes we are late

We speak back when insulted

We still work

We take days off

We call into work

We go on strike

We still work

10 days a week

Two jobs minimum

No overtime

Still getting paid for only 5

—For even less now

We still work

We work harder

Much harder

Get tired

Show up late

Call into work

Then return to work

Broke and broken

We work

And work

And Work

We work harder

Much harder than before

Then we die

We die broke

We die owing

Much more than before

We die more broken

We die much harder

—Fuck the national banks

Juan

Miguel

Milagros

Olga

Manuel

Are still dying

Juan is bribing local senators

Miguel lost the belt

Milagros disappeared

Olga sings of sadness

Manuel left for Broadway

They are all still dying

We die broken

In hurricanes

In earthquakes

Sin luz y aqua

In wars

From gunshots

In therapy

Traumatized

On drugs

And alcohol

Alone

Emotional and

Economic depressions

Are also tropical depressions

Let's talk about this

Aqui se habla Spanglish

—All the time

Aqui, they put America first

Aqui, they throw paper towels at us

Aqui, they call us all Mexican

Aqui, they call everyone immigrant

Aqui, we are all the same

Aqui, we are all non-white

Aqui, we are only brown

Aqui, we are the other

Aqui, to be called Latino

is to be unwelcomed.

POLLY ALICE

Rainbow Mandala

I dream of a barren plain
   under a rainbow.
   In the center of the circle
   are the slip tied tails
   of a single undulating ribbon.

   Knot, are you theory
   biting your
   tail end over end?
   You push the greyed
   dusk with a sword's edge,
   to a dream glow--

   Your beauty the destination
   of dreams the servant's back
   door to a serpentine path.

   Time, amuses you
   bridge to soul source, you
   make me certain

love is fifth dimensional.
Sift me
Universe-weaver
Until I'm a free-falling wonder
A flying, walking-on-water
invisible lasso throwing

Wonder because you've

set
me
free

not invincible, no armor
just the knowledge that
nothing here will last
and everything will

DONNA ISAAC

Entrepreneur Sans Wall

Across the border in the expectant night,
Ciudad Juarez sparkles like so many stars
beyond the desert darkness. An iron gate
encloses an ancient graveyard.
Alma and her son make a nightly raid
into El Paso to buy dozens of Krispy Kreme
donuts and then go back to sell
them from the trunk of her coche
to citizens who like plain glazed.
In the early morning hours,
customers might be drug dealers,
hookers, and hungry addicts, longing
for sugar, a lick of raspberry jam. They pay
pesos and/or dollars for the sticky goods.
Alma makes pennies on the dollar
so that her children can take classes
at Vista or the community college,
so that their abuela can buy masa and meat
for tamales she sells at Christmas,
so that they can feed their yellow dog
tied up, bones showing, in a yard filled with old tires.

MICHELLE BROOKS

Retain This Copy for Your Records

I am a room after everyone has left.
  Emptied out, you are free to imagine
  anything could happen. There's a song
  playing, the sound so faint that you
  can't tell where it's coming from
  and the vending machines offer all
  the candies you remember from childhood –
  Fifth Avenue Bars, Milky Ways, Whatchamacallits.
  In front of all this proffered sweetness, you
  wonder if this is what dying feels like. You
  buy a candy bar, sit down on the floor, and surrender
  to the ghosts because it's all that you can think to do.

Border Town

You're on Speaker

The story I can tell isn't dramatic. I'm
   sure you can relate. It's about horrible
   things that happened to me, by me. It's
   about secrets, open and otherwise, all
   the ones I clutched so hard that my nails
   bit into my skin. I carried them like my
   life depended on it, and I forgot why,
   and I forgot what it was to be free of them.
   They rattled inside me, and nothing bad
   happened, did it? I swallowed the evidence,
   and the evidence swallowed me. The world is
   lost, and I don't even know where to begin to look.

OMAR BÁRCENA

Linea Divisoria

Bitácora rota,
Itinerario escrito en lengua ajena

Traficábamos amor y cariño,
Nos creímos perseguidos

La división, no dividía esto,
Cortaba otras cosas,
Cortaba tiempo

Escaseaba el amor materno,
Apartaba a padre,
Y no era alcohol ni era puta.

Linea divisoria,
Que me cortas,
Que me atas las entrañas
Que magnificas lo insuficiente

Púas domables,
convertidas en cuchillas intocables

Me dicen que fue por amor,
Amor a crías, amor a patria,
Crear ventaja,
Ilusiones suplantando lo carente

Que regresaríamos,
Que acá no saben, que somos cálidos

Somo cálidos,
Cálidos como el ejercito del diablo,
Que en estas dunas vive,
Bajo esta tierra salada y fracturada
Somos cálidos,
Como llamas de estaca eterna

Somos cálidos,
Como el fuego que quema pestañas,
Como agua hirviendo, derramada sobre un mapa

Un mapa aun fresco
En el cual tinta disuelta
Cambio el lenguaje de este itinerario

Ahora se entiende la mancha,
Se a acomodado y calibrado.
En su propia deformidad,
Se a convertido en brújula adecuada
para estos nuevos rumbos, inseguros.
Tallados bien del cochambre que somos

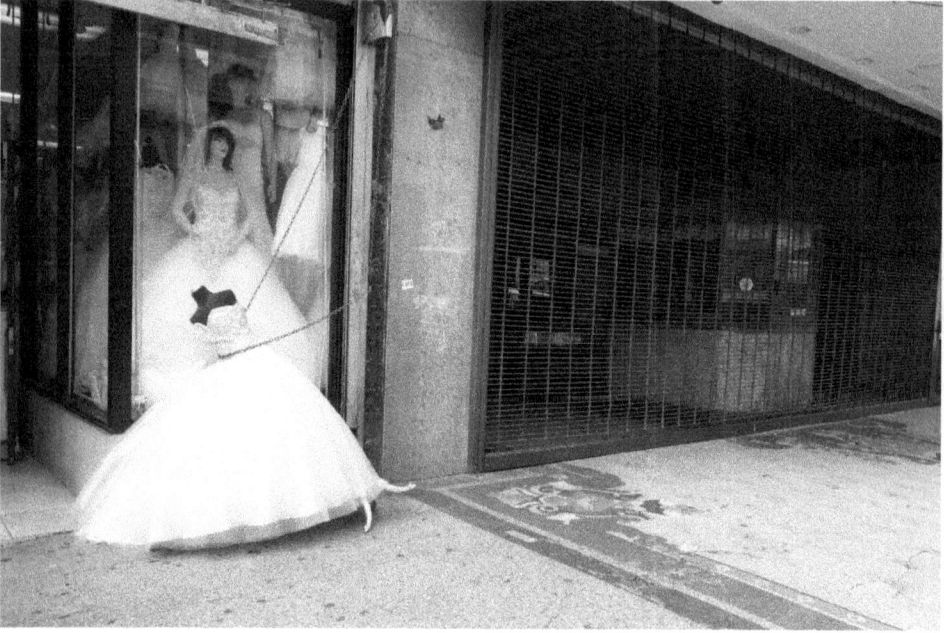

OMAR BÁRCENA

Fantasma de Quinceañera Encadenada

OMAR BÁRCENA

Mexicali-Calexico

Destino Manifiesto

Nos estamos convirtiendo en generaciones sin melancolía,
  A los cinco años
  Nos extirpan el hogar del pecho
  Nos dicen que hay patrias mejores,
  Que el soldado que en cada hijo te dio es mutable

  El constante sin hogar del labor de hoy,
  Hablamos en lenguas,
  Y nos acostumbramos a ver la tele sin doblar

  Al visitar re-aprendemos palabras,
  Que alguna vez escuchamos
  Pero que no practicamos

  Que hablar esta cosa era ventaja,
  Pero esta cosa, cargada de fachas
  Es la telaraña inescapable del nuevo destino manifiesto,
  El destino vertical de una reconquista

como una roca

comme une roche

like a rock

KATIE AFSHAR

The Escapists

My friend with the glossy
curls and grey eyes once
tried to save a relationship
by moving to the big island
with her lover. The locals
rejected the organic coffee
cart they'd built from scratch
and bullied the couple down
a dirt road. She found work
as a bar-girl, chatted up
customers, sipped between
smiles, leaving sticky lip
prints on the glass tumblers.

Of course, she fell in love with
another man—an old Hawaiian
who called her princess, like his
granddaughter. The two
competed for his attention while
the living room bustled in pit
bulls and paper plates soaked
with barbeque.

Back on this mainland when it was all
over, she told me her favorite part was
the clouds that hung out with the
island like best friends. I could feel
humid air when she said it, the frothy

shoreline, palm fronds wavering over
volcanic sand—I thought how I'd
grown skittish that year, always
checking my reflection in the rearview
as I drove, watching my inbox and the
blunt winter sky for signs of change.
So when I waited for the
mechanic to repair the clutch on
my old Toyota and spotted that
skinny kid in the mounted TV
 who jumped the chain link
at the San Jose airport
and stowed away in the wheel
well of a Hawaiian Islands
passenger plane I couldn't help
think as he stumbled over the
Maui tarmac stunned from oxygen
deprivation and below zero chill,
that I am seduced also by the
pretty lady painted on the fuselage
a plumeria behind her ear even up
against California's edge I want
the next edge a line of green
bumps way out in the Pacific
because what if I didn't leave
enough distance behind me?

ARACELI ESPARZA

At Dinner

In my black dress and her in her white dress//

She has her hair pinned

I have mine pressed//

Our eyes fixed

We sit/

Waiting/

Worried who will knock at the door,/

The timing will be perfect, their entry will be violent/

A raid/

I hold my papers, but she doesn't have any, so she holds my hand./

Audience Participation

My response to the not so new but televised ICE raids
11 PM on Feb. 9th 2018 on Twitter:

You want Chicana Poetry then listen to a niña's Corazón
breaking as their Mamí is getting patty wagoned out of town,
deportation the new mic drop?
#deportationspostmortum

Chicana reality is when your daughter is safe another
one is sleeping alone porque se llevaron su Mami
#migranightmares

Como la flor, fue tanto amor que se la arrancaron de su
corazón, y la tiraron otra a la tierra
#illegalpollentation

It's not enough to outlaw our tongue, they rip our
mothers away too.
#whatsthisworldhascometo

TARA CARNES
Options

When things get bad
   no one notices
   when I stay late at work
   teachers do that

   I practice piano for hours
   at my church job
   then sleep on crunchy old pew cushions
   the sanctuary quiet

   sometimes I stay with
   elderly choir members across the street
   through the blinds
   we watch my ex
   paw through the recycling bin
   and stomp around our porch

   my best friend's family
   shield me too
   and keep for me
   an extra toothbrush and contact solution

Mater

When things get really bad
   I slip into chapel
   and talk to Mater

   curled at the end of the pew
   in her quiet alcove
   I feel safe

   the hum of traffic
   and the clatter of students
   fades away

   warm sunlight
   streams through
   the jeweled colors
   of Mater's window

   I love her pink gown
   crown of stars
   and the way her head is
   bowed and listening

I close my eyes like hers

and know that
she understands despair

how it feels
to see your child
being hurt
and not being able to stop it

I beg her
again
please keep my baby safe
give me strength
to
hang
on

SAMANTHA MALAY

House 6

JULIE A. SELLERS

Noche de bachata

Tómame la mano
and we'll dance,
pegaditos,
feet tracing the patterns
drawn by our hearts.
The bongó pulses in time
to broken corazones
while the primera guitarra
cries our misfortunes
in bittersweet droplets,
and the güira scrapes soft sighs
of impossibilities
as segunda y bajo
weave the fabric of our souls' desires.

Una noche de bachata,
a night of amargue,
to live this sentimiento
step by step,
spinning and turning,
vuelta tras vuelta,
contrary to the relentless pulse of time.

So, take my hand,
bailemos,
one last dance,
drawn by this visceral magnet
of raw emotion,
amargue,
this blues that joins us
on the edge,
al borde,
al filo
of goodbye.

VICCI JACOBS

Spange

Spare any change? I whisper as I stumble
  along Decatur Street. The words taste
  strange on my tongue,
  but I hate it here and I'm scared.

I need to get on that Greyhound
  so I can get the hell out of 'Nola.

They all walk by so fast.
  The smell of gumbo
  and spicy creole shrimp, the sweet scent of beignets,
  all drifting along with them.

Do I even exist?

Years later, as I start entering my car
  a man will ask me the same question,
  can you spare some change?
  I'll jump,

not because of him, but because
  I won't notice anyone around me.
  He'll step back with his hands
  up to show innocence. Please don't be scared of me.

I'll want to scream,
  I'm one of you.

But, I won't be.

I'll touch his hand as I rummage
through my purse. Some part of me will want to show him,
that despite my clean jeans and new car,
I'm not so different,

or, maybe,

I'll just want to prove to myself
that I haven't changed that much.

KEVIN CALLAHAN
The Supplicant

EVAMARIA LUGO

Notas De Amor

Necesito escribir notas de amor para ella y esconderlas debajo de la almohada en la noche y dentro de mi cuaderno de dibujo en la mañana. Protegida por la tradición que me sostiene, inocentemente escribo paz, benevolencia, alegría... y podría de igual manera decir: el desierto, las montañas, niños, música, el color azúl, su nombre antes de nacer. Y me encuentro a mi misma aquí, en el centro de la ciudad, tomando café, otra vez dibujando y escribiendo. Ansio crear una vida de amor y belleza para ella pero en realidad solo poseo este momento.

Love Notes

I need to write love notes to her and hide them under the pillow at night and inside my sketchbook in the morning. Protected by the tradition that sustains me, I innocently write peace, benevolence, joy... and I could just as well say the desert, mountains, children, music, the color blue, her name before she was born. And I find myself here, downtown, drinking coffee, writing and drawing again. I long to create a lifetime of love and beauty for her but in reality, I just own this moment.

JANET POWERS

Japanese China

The china was exquisite,
  pale blue dishes edged
  with tiny peach blossoms,
but we were on a pueblo
in the middle of New Mexico
and they didn't seem to match
the bead-draped deer's head
on the wall and the fry bread
served for breakfast.

"Tell me about your plates,"
I said, "there must be a tale,"
and of course there was,
a sad one, the set a gift
from a Japanese family,
forced into a camp during
a war when we didn't
trust each other not to lie
or attack from within.

"They gave everything away,"
she explained, "but my mother
lived nearby and talked often
with her Japanese friend
about how our people were
hounded by the Spanish first
and then the US government."
Because of stories shared,
precious plates were given.

Strange how history circles round,
bringing us again to that place
where we do not trust, and speak
of deportation and building walls.
Just yesterday a restaurant closed,
its waiters sent to Mexico,
and we the poorer for it:
the gift was in the salsa
and the chimichangas.

MEGAN WILDHOOD

Adulto

En

   mi pequeñez,
   pensé que todo

   estaba atrapado,
   fuerte y alto, nada se
   movería en el bosque de

   la memoria: todo es
   definitiva y permanente
   como los árboles centenarios,
   se mantuvieron sin cambiar hasta
   mi entrada en el claro desnudo del mundo.

MICHELLE BROOKS

Camp Bowie at Night

Working girls huddle in front
  of hotels, their burning cigarettes
  punctuating the night like fireflies,
  exclamation points that will be
  discarded without ceremony. Sinbad's,
  "The Classiest Strip Club with the Most
  Beautiful Girls," advertises an all you can
  eat buffet. It used to be a Red Lobster.
  My parents took my sister and me there
  to celebrate birthdays. I longed for a hot
  pink sequined tube top, sandals that turned
  into roller skates when you pushed a button
  on the cork-lined heel, a black silk robe to wear
  while listening to Grover Washington Jr's
  Winelight and drinking champagne. It's all
  different now. And yet the desire only morphs,
  never satiated. I stop at Walgreens, hear glass
  shatter somewhere in the night. When I return
  to my car, I see pieces of a pipe strewn
  about like confetti. It only held smoke
  so half-full or half-empty doesn't apply.

SAMANTHA MALAY

Parking Lot 4

ARACELI ESPARZA

Settle the Score II

He wanted to be that someone like they say
Some are born rich, I mean great
Some achieve a suburban home, I mean greatness,
And some have greatness shot at them, I mean murdered.
I knew that our people's love is a course that never did run
smooth.
I knew it and still until he died I didn't understand how this
fight was for our babies.
Our children, whose worth is consistently devalued,
dehumanized, defected.
Even by us.
I can't point a finger at anyone, but I will start in our own
back yard of– putting toys before time,
My crooked ass ways, halfway parenting, and giving up
before giving a shit.
Oh, but I'm not supposed to write about that, because
weren't we also children?
When lil Johnny got shot? Or Sheena, Or Alex?
And the list goes on, on and on.
But why didn't we stop it? Why couldn't we stop it? We had
Rodney, we had even Arsenio!
Yep, but we didn't have us.
...
Some youth are blinded into thinking this isn't about race,
class or gender.
Some of them have stopped listening.
Some of them believe they are safe.

ELOÍSA PÉREZ-LOZANO
Mutant

I look like you, but I'm not quite like you
   hiding in plain sight, another me waits
   for the right moment.

   English easily lobs between us
   when my phone interrupts
   just a second, I say.

   I hear Mamá's voice and I morph
          you look up, thoughtful
                  as my inner form appears.

               A few notches louder than before
               my mellifluous melody charms you
               with its Mexican rhythm and beat

        But I didn't come to confuse, only entrance
        in linguistic dance, a bilingual romance

With you I am an English master
then, in a second, I've switched
she's gone...

Y ahora estoy aquí
and you are lost in a maze
unfamiliar with my turns of phrase

Consonantes crujientes y vocales abiertas
are tendrils from my tongue, luring
your ears to drown in sensuous sonidos

Ni sabes lo que oyes, but you're hypnotized
stunned into speechlessness under my spell
a deer in a daze, petrified by palabras.

I say "Adios, Mamá" and the spell is broken
my English returns with the girl you know.

No longer needed, my nature retreats
the outer veneer in place once more…
You won't remember, but I'll never forget

The way your eyes saw my other side
glimpsed at that reality
and didn't recognize me.

I grin from inside, waiting for the next time
I catch you unawares.

como un pájaro

comme un oisea

like a bird

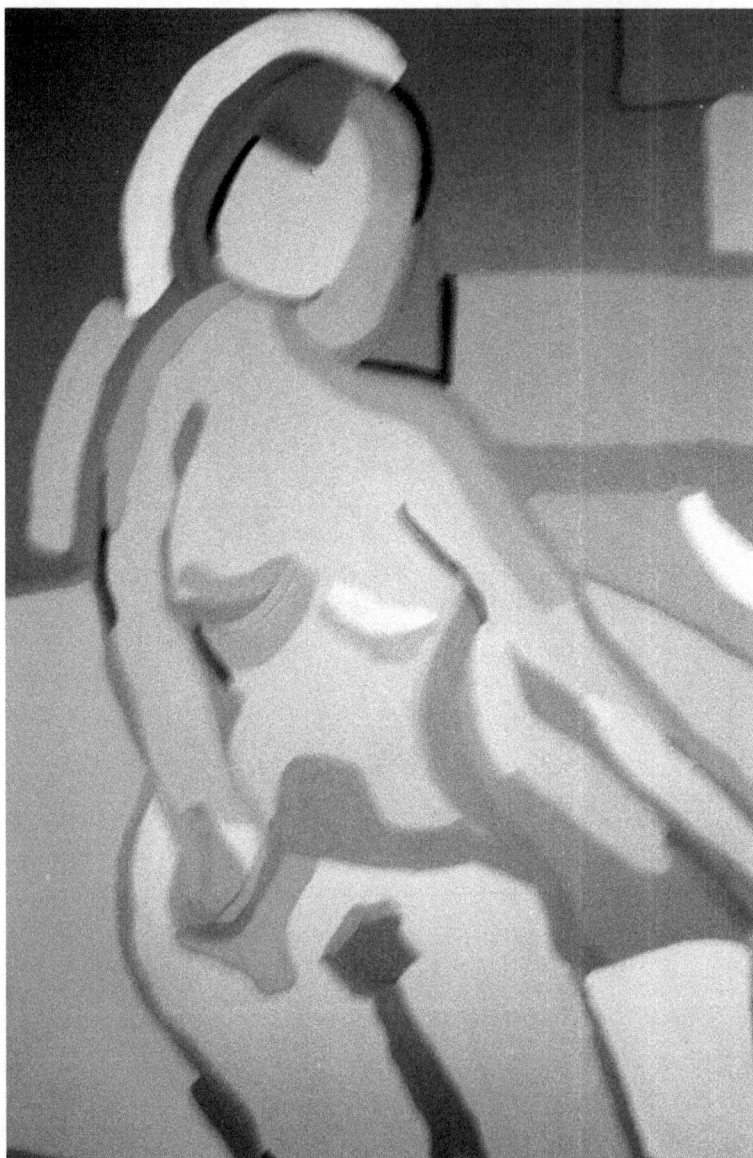

LUGO

What I Own

A. KAISER

Velvet Shell

Calcareous transparent pink shell powdery skin solely along its minute revolving striae.

The closest to a velvet ear you can be – seaside among stones, near low tide.

You lie in listening wait behind a veil – foam, froth and spume.

The velvet, easily lifted and unwound, will have you fall to pieces.

A. KAISER

The Lady

Of Guadalupe is
  in our basement.
  Framed against the wall,
  floating across deep green and blue spaces.
  I was arranging one more time,
  personal effects

  —

  still
  living out of unzipped bags
  reaching blind
  searching for my things, my things, my
  things.
  Paying back the universe for my other life
  as a regentrifier
  when she appeared.
  Painted by my brother who,
  with emptiness as his landscape,
  even denies himself sleep
  walking in a
  bubble
  he can't burst
  wishing he was this mountain backdrop:
  so sure and tall;
  wishing he was this cloud of peace:
  so smooth and wide.

A. KAISER

Crown

A. KAISER

In Wait

I was alone. How could I not be? -Louise Glück

I feel it alone on this
crowded earth. How
could I not be lying as I
was next to my returned
sleeping husband?

For years I went about my days
trusting I was not calling
attention. The smooth, bare
wood of the spool I exposed and
hid, wound and unwound in
turn.

Such a homebody to have chosen
a man whose presence felt like
absence. Departure, foreign lands
and women winding in his veins.
I loved my home.

In between the threads' warp and weft
before so many
opportune eyes I tried, also, to mother
our fatherless one,
hands idle curbed
back to the shore.

The surprise was the return. We
had gotten so used to his leaving
only the dog sniffed him for who
he was while, huddled in the
corner, we watched.

because I teach them to sew and everything
Stiff white linen offset our forest honey coated
teeth. You there again between beats of the
heart, thrusting.

Against the ironwork palms of hands wetted.
Open doors and starch. Stretched over hips,
yearning.

Retracing out of the question with his tongue
down her throat and a nun looking adrift
blowing by.

Whoever's reading through the pane's
reading too loudly groping her forgotten
rhythms.

Black-clothed villagers travel back roads,
mistaking known with unknown, stars
for creation.

Surprised how shining birds led their
sandaled feet to the sea's jagged edge,
bound by wire.

She echoes the reverberation underneath.
Dust- veiled, she falters amid their
makeshift murmurs.

When she puts ear to water, back to the sky, she
hears *they love me because I teach them to sew
and everything.*

JILL BRONFMAN

Eileen y Guadalupe

BRUCE PRATT

Laughter

Le rire.	The laugh.
J'aurais souri,	I would have smiled,
Mais Je me souviens	But I recall
Une etreinte froide.	A bitter embrace.
Le recul du orgueil	The recoil of hubris,
Le ravisseur	The abductor
De mon peur	Of my fear
Une fracture, une sortie.	A fracture, an exit.
Le gage de la promesse	The token of promise,
Un cri d'un assassin	An assassin's cry.
Pour arrosser le jardin	To water the garden
De l'herbes fines est mortelles	Of deadly herbs.

MEGAN WILDHOOD

El Fin de Dia

En casa después del trabajo
  Mi hijo estába silbando
  los perros estaban ladrando

  Una puesta del sol en el cielo
  tararea, los niños cubrir la tierra en juego

  durantemuchos años
  perdí esta música

  la espera de la vida real
  para irrumpir en todo

  pero cuando el sol
  desaparece por la noche

  y los grillos armonizan en el suave atardecer,
  recuerdo de nuevo

  que sólidos son los sonidos de la vida

ARACELI ESPARZA

My Rib Cage

Encircles a fish called
  She-lung.
  My She-lung is a fish
  She is a glowing orange,
  green with flecks of red
  with a scaly cascading fins
  her long and curly eye lashes break open.
  A She-lung:
  Longs for ocean
  Calls for a reunification of the present
  moment and her body
  after she hears,
  "Those colored people."

KRISTIN GALLAGHER

Wrong Limb (Brink of despair)

Woman who thinks she is nice
   feeds birds buckets of birdfeed—
   til morning before Christmas when
   she goes south
   for the winter.

   Ten below zero. Fifteen.
   Birds perch in empty trees,
   praying to her deaf door to open.

   I too have sat in wrong tree,
   praying for wrong door
   to open.

The Very Edge (Edge of uncertainty)

A verge I tremble on
   a precipice I might fall off—
   a mountain ridge…
   a ledge to fledge
   the eaglet
   in this chick.

A. KAISER

The Twitching Blind

The long light curtains
   tug across the unsteady rod
   set on the paint-encrusted nails
   already there
   when I moved in.

   to keep the light out
   a maroon airplane throw
   from an extinct company
   too decent to last –
   layered on.

   I'll leave the window
   ajar – up in the loft bed
   it can get so hot – push in
   my earplugs. Make void
   garbage pick-up at 4 am

   and all night long
   the twitching blind.

ERIC MACHAN HOWD

The Piano

there is that moment of clarity when the shoe toes the
pedal
when the knot can be tied unconsciously while humming
the tune

countenances disappearing into the crowded hall
that time when all is black and white and the right hand
brings out melody and phrase

                                                    teeth lost in alley fight

hearing Beethoven for the first time, the roofer lets
his hammer weigh his hand down to the pitch
a bucket of ten-penny nails full of rusty jigs and reels
sounds of the spheres depressing and releasing the fingers

the curve of the outside of an ear blackened in the fire of
sentimentality
wind arranges wind
                three strings vibrate with each other pulse in common time
the student practices on keyboard with an orange under each palm

used uprights and spinets practice mindfulness in landfills
the key is pressed   the note speaks true

a Union soldier shot in the thigh regards the woman holding her finger

on his artery

after hearing the chord he tells her that she can let go

it is the dampers that create the silences in music

what is first touched must be absolved

the sounding board cracked long ago

the crooked smile of old ivory keys

                        that one sound without

            strings

percussive emotion

          John Cage's *Four thirty-three* in three movements

the silence before the tears of a child disappointed

          moments

when the white space crescendos over black characters

on the page

left intentionally blank

JEFFREY HANTOVER

Pu'uhonua o Honaunau (Place of Refuge)

They came in the days of the gods
   the vanquished the victims of hate
   the *kapu* breakers
   whose innocent shadows fell on royal stones
   who stepped across the sacred lines
   that marked the hours of their lives
   all found absolution on this sacred ground.

   We struggle against the waves
   to keep afloat in chilly water
   and head for the rocky shore
   no priests bless us
   no ceremonies cleanse us
   only love given and received
   the sacred ground
   beneath our feet
   where no questions are asked
   where there is always a second chance.

MEGAN WILDHOOD

En la Pradera

Comenzé el voluntariado en los Sabados
  Plantando arboles
  Y recogerando la basura.

  Una vez que las latas de cerveza y bolsas
  De plástico fueron despejados – la tierra realmente
  Es maravillosa tal como se hizo la primera vez –

  Nosotros de tacón nuestras palas en ella
  Y excavamos casitas nuevas
  Para la más majestuosa de todas las criaturas.

  Y, por estas horas fugaces en el sudor y la suciedad,
  No importa tanto que
  La tierra es un movimiento de arena.

G. WISE

Luger, 1948

I remember the room

its criss-cross patterned wallpaper

crowded, cluttered with scarred furniture

trophies, a boy's room, two beds

brothers, I was ten

and I remember the flash

the impossibly loud crack

and gunsmoke or residue

and the boy holding the

Luger he'd pointed at my head

his older brother's pistol

and the hole in the

wall behind me

plaster, lath, torn

open especially

where the bullet

exited

the wall

after it

scorched the

criss-crosss

All was quiet
but a ringing
in my ears.

"I didn't know it was loaded,"
the kid said. I think his
brother beat him up
when he found out.

The bullet went next door.

After it
ZINNNGED
past my head.
I remember.

So far I've lived
another
seventy
years.

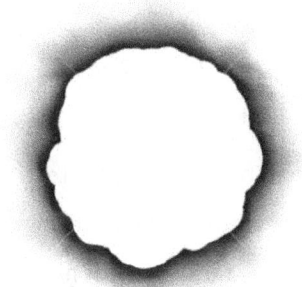

JEFFREY HANTOVER

7:30 A.M. September 11, 2001

The world is not yet awake.
   At J&J Harmony Cleaners on University
   a young man cradles a light green short-sleeve corduroy shirt
   white fluff like the hair in an old man's ear
   puffs from the placket

   Can you fuse or glue it?
   Don't stitch it, it will show.

   The man behind the counter
   half way through the morning's first cup
   smoothes the shirt with his hand
   says he'll try.

It's irreplaceable
if you can't, don't try
I'll take it to the man
who makes my suits.

He pauses at the door
turns around
for one last look
at the shirt
like an only child
gurneyed through the emergency room doors
Be careful
it's irreplaceable
and he heads downtown

Hamlet Watches Tai-Chi

A prince among platypuses
   peeks from my daughter's backpack.

   Old woman back straight as bamboo
   bends one leg then the other
   on the green hillside
   half swallowed by morning fog
   her body paints characters
   stroke by stroke in the air
   with outstretched arms
   she embraces the world.

   The boys clamber over the monkey bars
   while the school nurse talks to the girls
   in their blue and green jumpers
   their clunky black shoes
   about "their changes"
   the budding breasts
   the blood
   they whisper about at recess.

   She climbs onto the school bus
   without looking back.
   I walk up the steep driveway
   to the morning paper
   to a day that will never come again.

POLLY ALICE

The Path of Birds

Snow,
  Blast you!
  You and your
  feathers of frost
  Your strangling
  hands around the
  neck of the creek
  until his teeth chatter

Snow,
  You sloth!
  You and your
  creeping crawl
  Your precious
  pinkie finger holds
  back the clock
  until she's slower

Snow...
  What's that—
  small tracks...
  of tiny sparrows
  and here a
  rabbit.
  Awe—
  how precious

Snow,
  You Dear!
  You and yours
  laid bare. Your
  crisp wafers
  reveal the path
  of birds until
  they fly

Neige,
  Je vous déteste!
  —vos plumes de givre
  Vos mains étranglantes
  les mains autour du cou
  du ruisseau jusqu'a
  ce que ses dents claquaient
  avec de froid

Neige,
  Vous paresse!
  —votre rampant
  lentement
  votre doigt de petit
  précieux retient l'horloge
  jusqu'a ce qu'elle soit
  plus lente

Neige...
  Ce qui est cela—
  des empreintes mingnon
  de moineaux petites
  et ici...
  un lapin.
  Adorable—
  comment précieux.

Neige,
  Vous Cher!
  Vous et les votres
  mis à nu—vos hosties
  croquantes reverent
  le chemin d'oiseaux
  jusqu'a ce qu'ils
  volent

ANNE WHITEHOUSE

Lightning Strike

I

The house lay drowsing in the late afternoon,
a cooling shade crept across the valley,
punctuated by the crow's harsh caws
as it landed briefly, rose up, and flew away.

From room to room I lingered,
caressing the door jambs, the walls,
in gratitude to Providence
for saving us from lightning's strike.

I'd rarely seen a more even cut
than the one that split the Norway spruce,
when lightning shriveled its living sap,
and woke us with a thunderclap,

raining wooden arrows and stripped bark.
A board sawed cleanly as a two-by-four
hurled to earth, tearing up the hostas.
High in the tree, another perched perilously.

Lightning jumped inside the propane tank,
and the fireplace heater roared into flame,
as loud as wind, gushing black smoke that stank,
while we fled in a daze, and the firemen came.

                        II

The creature must have slipped inside unnoticed,
through the open door that stormy night,
as the firemen were moving their equipment,
their lights a tunnel from darkness to darkness,

and everything else was shadow and rain
falling quietly after the fire was put out.
Within that shadow moved another, never noted,
not knowing where it was, or how to leave.

All else was shadow and the sound of rain,
after the lightning died away, and the fire was put out,
only the sound of the rain was left
softly falling to earth, and at last we slept.

III

They are manuring the field next to us.
Inhale, exhale: odor of animal,
signs of cultivation, the life cycle.

Two nights past the fire, loud scufflings
disturb my rest; on the third,
I am startled as a wild, black bird
soars up the stairs in panicked flight
and orbits my head like a planet out of whack—

a trapped, lost bird that came in by mistake
and now wants out. To show the way,
I go down first, flick on the lights,
fling open the door, "This way to freedom,
it's so close, if you can only see it."

And the bird flies out the front door at last.

comme le soleil

como el sol

like the sun

MALCOLM GLASS

The Land I

In the land behind, beyond

nowhere, no flags fly, no
fences march along the worn

dirt ruts of country lanes,
and windows no longer hold
the waning faces of the moon.

KEVIN CALLAHAN

Anza Borego

The amber dawn slants across
worn footprints of beetles,
caterpillars, red horned spiders.
Boreal winds thread the empty

branches of dwarf hornbeams
and Chinese elms. Nameless,
numberless stars and their
planets, wrapped in clouds,
ringed with rock, bear witness.

A zenith of condors soars
in spirals, their feathers trailing
mist from the snow on a lost
mountain range. Their pale
sanguine wings churn

cauldrons of clouds, daphne
blue against the ivory sky.
As umber dusk sinks over the
vacant eyes of the fallen

stone figures on the horizon,
a flock of sable beaucerons
and border collies follow a herd

of sheep down a parched
stream bed, casting before them

the copper music of bells.

ANNE WHITEHOUSE

Meteor Shower

We lie on blankets in the grass
   grateful for the scratchy wool
   in the sudden chill of night
   deep within the virgin forest
   at a family reunion far from our homes.

   Scanning the sky for falling stars—
   there goes one! and there another!
   Persistent trains, bright fireballs—
   in the great immensity
   a crescent moon crosses to Jupiter,

   and snatches of conversation fly up
   more intimate now
   we are hidden in darkness
   and can express what
   we might not say otherwise.

At every instant we are
what we have been and will be,
our forebears who live on in us
we remember, we resemble.

Everything in the world is mysterious
formed of tenuous substances
evanescence and oblivion
the equivocal element of time.

With a stone I dug up a clod of dirt
a little farther away I laid it down silently
and under my breath I whispered
"*I have changed the earth.*"

The deed was minimal, the words exact,
and I needed a lifetime to say them.

ANNE WHITEHOUSE
Dancing In Water

for Eiko and Koma

A frame of driftwood
in the current's ebb and flow—
clinging to the frame,
the dancers, stiff as driftwood,
curve slowly into stones
while water runs over
their stilled forms.

In time they come alive,
are rippling reeds,
swaying stem and buried root,
variously wind, tree,
flower, naked breath
that swells behind
the push to give birth.

The dancers are in the river,
the dance is in the river,
the dance is the river.

From outside in I found this story:
she almost died,
and he brought her back to life.

Dried leaves, discarded and scattered—
let them go; new ones will grow.
A cricket perched on a twig,
graceful and humorous
at the close.

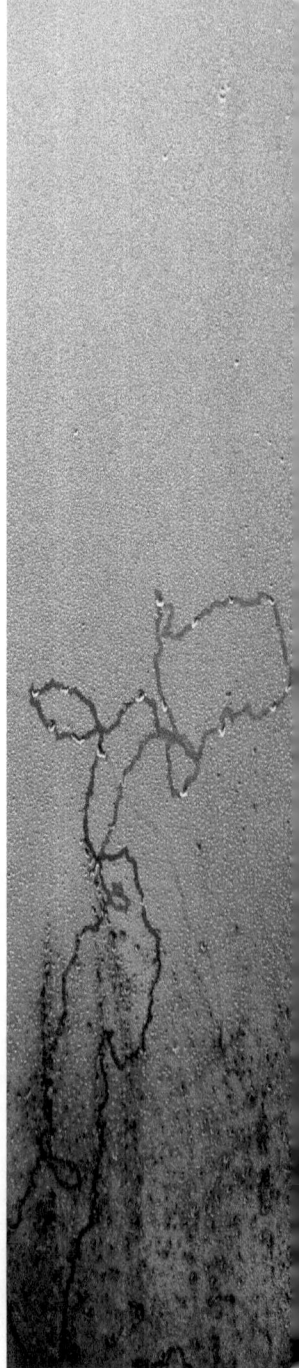

MICHELLE BROOKS

Notre Dame Is Burning

You left months ago, and I became
    a ghost, haunting my own life for clues
    about how nothing changes until it does.
    We are left with ashes, and my heart burns
    and I don't know if I will ever not feel it.
    The firefighters in Paris saved some
    of the statues, and many were removed
    for restoration, removed on wires, the glorious
    saints flying through the air to another destination.

    Without you, my life is a salvage yard,
    and I wander through the shadows, like
    the ones that flicker on the television,
    watching the all-consuming fire. When
    they announce that they have saved
    the crown of thorns, I think *That sounds right.*

POLLY ALICE

metro stop communion

In a dark gallery
   train storms echo
   and roll through
   people closed
   people open
   breathe
   a girl with
   red hair's been
   sitting arms
   around her
   knees
   crying next to the
   tracks.

... *doors open*

together at last
two women embrace
greet after a long time

... *doors closing*

a man with universe-
night skin sits near the
blind man
in his white trench coat

... *doors open*

flashbulbs pop
stars sizzle
escalators snake
silently under
a dark gallery
where there
is no sky but us

MANO SOTELO

Accountability Polarity and Separation

HUASCAR MEDINA, KANSAS POET LAUREATE

"New American" — The Konza Poetry Project Presents:
Somewhere Between Kansas City and Denver

<u>New American</u>

Don't call me immigrant
   I am the New American
   striving in New America
   as a New American
   I am not your invader
   not an animal
   nor criminal
   I am a just person
   just striving
   in a New America

   In New America I am
   a full-time student
   overtime worker
   volunteering in my free time
   if I plan enough ahead for free time
   if I can even afford the free time
   if my free time is approved

   I work hard in New America
   3rd shift warehouse
   2nd shift my house
   always on call
   no days off
   freelance for life

4 jobs a week
blue and white collar

Don't call me immigrant
I am the New American
surviving in New America
as a New American
I am not your invader
not an animal
nor criminal
I am a just person
just surviving
in a New America

This is New America
student loans for all
high rent
higher utilities
low pay
rising healthcare costs
the cost of living
—deadly
no living wage
living enraged
my cousins encaged

for wanting to live in
a safer part of
New America

Don't call me immigrant
I am the New American
living in New America
as a New American
I am not your invader
not an animal
nor criminal
I am a just person
just living
in a New America

Strong and proud
able to withstand
the distance I have traveled
the distance from my family
the distance between us
the distance of our dialects
the distance in our churches
the distance in our homes
the distance between my ancestors
and my grandchildren
the distance from the streets
to the dorm rooms
the distance from the field
to the corner office suite

Don't call me immigrant
I am the New American
dreaming of New America

as a New American
I am not your invader
not an animal
nor criminal
I am a just person
just dreaming
of a New America

Old America
don't be afraid
we are all America
North America
Central America
South America
We are all Americans
We all strive in Americas
We all survive in Americas
We all live in Americas
They are all the same America

We all dream of a greater America
I want you to be paid a living wage
live in affordable housing
without college debt
or medical debt
or credit card debt
or national debt
I want no more racism
I am speaking of a New America
I am part of New America
whether you like it or not
so join me, please

como la montaña

comme la montagne

like the mountain

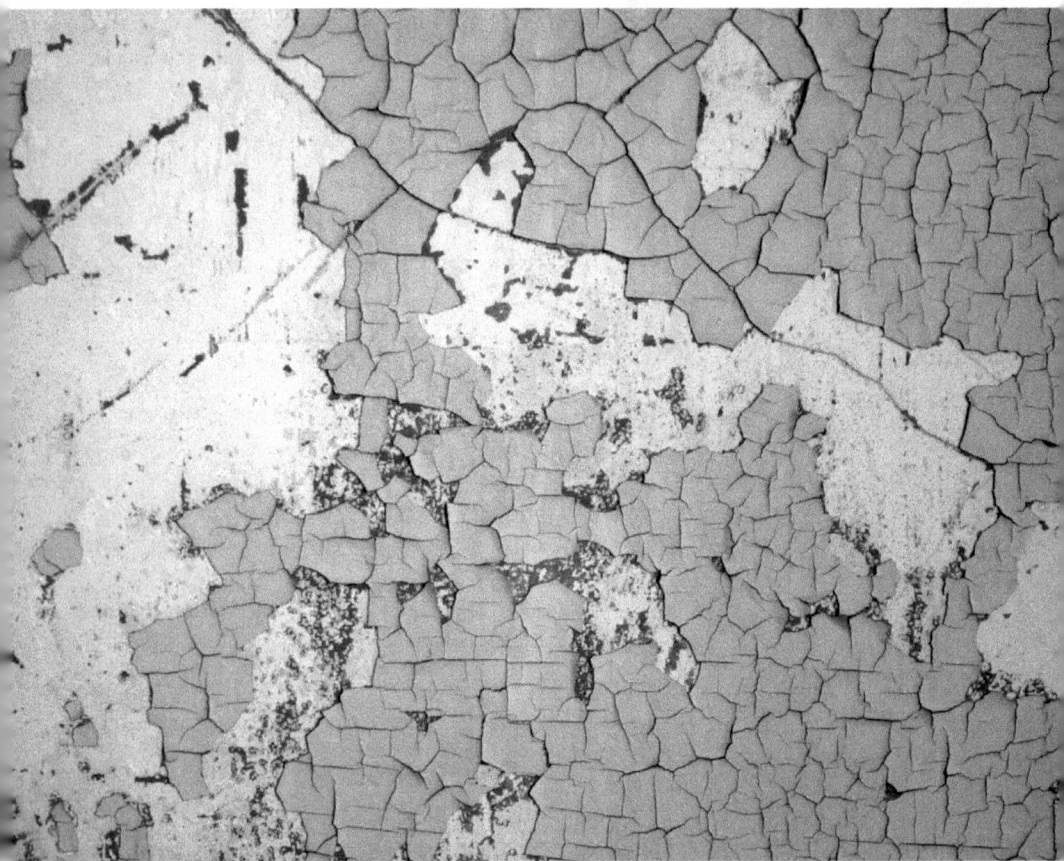

KEVIN CALLAHAN

Wall, Alcatraz

J. WEINTRAUB

All My Dead

All my dead came home to me that night.
  My father seemed taller than he'd been, before
  his cancer had tamed him, turned him frail and worn.
  Eyes once chalked with cataracts were bright.
  He didn't smile, but never smiled much when alive,
  and yet he seemed pleased to be alive once more.
  Uncles, aunts, and cousins, too, had all arrived
  with those forgotten ones whose names I'd find
  on yellowed cards and letters left behind
  in those drawers so full of memories, retrieved
  from my parents' empty home. I believed
  it was a family affair or holiday,
  for across the room on the other side
  was the favorite aunt of my wife, who'd died
  too young, my father-in-law, at ease, arrayed
  in his finest, as always cool, remote,
  yet expectant, awaiting my approach;
  but as I crossed to greet them, the first dim rays
  of early morning summer filtered through
  the window, pierced them through, as if they, too,
  had been made of glass, as transparent as air,
  dissolving them without the trace
  of a shadow lingering, before I could share
  a final word, a last embrace.

CÉCILE OUMHANI

Poet's Residency In The French Alps

1

Qui entend la ville
pliages de papier
égrenés au bord d'un ruban
à la merci du vent et de la pluie
au fond de la vallée

limpide l'œil de l'oiseau
épris de ses falaises de pierre

le ciel sera-t-il assez clair
pour déchiffrer l'histoire de la terre
au miroir des neiges oubliées
près de troncs silencieux?

2

De quelles contrées rêve la neige
endormie loin dans sa ravine

elle a tant tournoyé dans l'inconnu
goûté au vertige du ciel
après l'errance des nuages
engrangé couleurs et reflets
en prévision des étés à venir
des bouts d'étoiles ont fait sa couche

oubliée à l'ombre des rochers
elle attend l'ivresse du torrent
et la promesse du sol

3

Coutumier des ermitages
le pin a fait vœu de silence

suspendu à la falaise
dont il a fait son oratoire
rare silhouette arrimée
à sa miette de terre
année après année
il contemple le vide
où disparaît la vallée
pluies ou tempêtes
peu lui importe

l'immensité du ciel
est son ravissement
la légèreté de l'heure
l'infini de son chemin

© Kēvin Callahan

ALAN DUNNETT

Shot in the Head

It saddens me these bodies remain
for so long on the ground. We are afraid

to move them. My hair turns white and I say
to my husband, I've been shot. I'm dripping

with blood. Look! And he is very still
in our night, unafraid, unlike me,

to step out into the street. A little
boy comes to the house and says you must leave.

You lock yourself in and listen to guns
and soon they will come and break down the door.

You have a house, they threaten you, you leave,
They take the house.
        I go with the children

and my husband's ghost. In another town,
we rest but there too I hear them singing.

Inspired by *Throwing Stones At The Moon:*
Narratives from Colombians
Displaced by Violence – Voice of Witness

JILL BRONFMAN

Grand-daughter

I step up to the podium
   I lift my bell-bottomed jeans to meet me
   Slide my thick glasses up the bridge of my nose
   I begin

   My mother came to this country
   My grandmother came to this country
   My great-grandmother came to this country
   And each time, they came back for me
   Before that
   I do not know
   But what I do know
   Is that I like my foremothers
   Have come to this country
   To speak

   I speak in Spanish, and Portuguese
   And Czech and Hindi

   I speak in riddles and love songs
   For the ones I have left behind
   My children
   My parents
   My fields of corn, and cotton

My pigs, cows, and sheep
Weaving, pots thrown, and pots on the fire
Please meet me this time
Meet me in the middle
And not just by noses
Pushed through fat steel fingers

Meet me in the middle
Of our thoughts

Mi preciosa
My child, this country
I was not born into
But that I birthed myself

ANNE WHITEHOUSE

One Summer Day On The Number One Train

When the doors of the express opened at 72 Street,
   the local was waiting. She entered with me,
   tall and angular as a crane, her expression alert,
   violin poised against her clavicle like a wing.

The train was half-empty, the passengers dozing
   or absorbed in their smartphones.
   She stood at one end of the car, her gaze
   swiftly appraising us, while the doors slid shut.

Closing her eyes, she lifted her bow
   and dipped her chin, and into that pause
   went all the years of preparation
   that had brought her to this moment.

The train accelerated in a rush of cacophony,
   her music welled up, and I recognized
   a Bach concerto blossoming to fullness
   like an ever-opening rose. Suddenly

I was crying for no reason and every reason,
   in front of strangers. I thought of the courtroom
   where, an hour ago, I'd sat listening to testimony
   with fellow jurors, charged to determine the facts
   and follow the law. But no matter how we tried,

we couldn't reverse damage or undo wrong.
The music was contrast and balm, like sunlight
in subterranean air. The tears wet on my cheeks,

I broke into applause, joined by fellow passengers.
We'd become an audience, her audience,
just before the doors opened and we scattered.
Making my offering, I exited, too shy to catch her eye.

But she'd seen the effect her music had wrought.
Its echo resounded in my memory, following me
into the glory of the summer afternoon.
It is with me still.

ANNE WHITEHOUSE

THE "E-E-E-E-E-E"

The sound could be long and drawn out
   like a hissing wind—
   e-e-e-e-e-e-e-e—
   or short and staccato
   like eruptions from the gut—
   eee-eee-eee-eee-eee.
   I don't know how it started
   among us four siblings
   but I know how it grew.
   It sounded like so many things—
   fear, enthusiasm, excitement—
   but what it really meant was danger.

   We thought it kept us safe
   but in the end
   it prevented us from saying
   what we wanted to tell each other.
   I think we were afraid
   we would speak truths
   that we could not unsay
   about our parents and ourselves,
   and love would vanish like evaporation.
   And so one of us would go,
   e-e-e-e-e, and another
   would pick it up and carry it
   like a round to the next.

The themes and variations
kept us going for years.
It meant everything,
and it meant nothing—
our secret childhood language
unleashed of words—
an unbearable sorrow
without explanation.

SAMANTHA MALAY

Night Bloom #13

KĒVIN CALLAHAN

Across the Universe

In the deep dark of near midnight, early spring sticks icy
    fingers probing the edges of my jacket
    Illumination from millions of stars in a cloudless sky,
    a night light shimmering from horizon to horizon

    Settled on a stump sticking through the soil of a bare farm lot,
    I sit pensively smoking, contemplating the canopy overhead

    Tonight, my happy task is being nurse to thirteen brood
    sows birthing their babes in wriggling bunches
    Inside the farrowing house expectant mothers lay in
    private pens just large enough to lay down
    and not crush their newborn brood

    Moist air is redolent of fresh straw warmed
    by heat lamps hung over each space
    One-by-one babes slide into their new universe, covered in mucus
    I scoop them up wipe them clean introduce them to momma's breasts

    Clutching each wriggling body close to my face
    I inhale the sweet sweet perfume
    Never, before or since, have I taken in the aroma
    of anything like a newborn baby porker
    Soft grunts escape tiny bodies when,
    instinctively they find their first meal

At times babies become blocked in the birth canal
In those critical moments I morph into an obstetrician,
reach inside, grasp and extract the babe, alive
What does it mean to be responsible
helping to bring this much life into the world?
Watching/assisting new life move from one universe into another

I am seventeen, in a few minutes, I will be one day closer
to eighteen, entering into a new life
Tonight, my world exists/has existed within this dome of
light enveloping me from horizon to horizon and scant further

Gazing into the glittering galaxies above, I muse,
"There has to be more than this,"
Questions about the future niggle like cold fingers, probing, asking
"What must be out there in that vast space/that place yet undiscovered?"

Time passed for me as it does for us all
Soon enough I ventured out to explore other universes,
so many places unknown to me
A wonderful journey that coincidentally came full circle years later

On a warm spring day, I brought my wife and sons back to the farm
They watched as I leapt the fence to assist
in another live birth of baby pigs, an echo of my past

Yes, far from a cold empty farm lot I have traveled

But, that boy-not-yet-man, the warm lamp glow that fought

off the cold, the soft grunts of babies and mommas, the

sweet, sweet perfume of new life stays with me always

on my journey from there to now — Across the Universe

comme la noche

comme la nuit

like the night

KEVIN CALLAHAN

Darkness Abates

ANNE WHITEHOUSE

Mothers Of Suicides

The mothers of the suicides
wear downcast looks years later.
The skin of their faces sag,
the corners of their mouths are etched
in expressions of permanent discontent,
hollows of sadness form around their eyes.

Their sons took their lives at home,
in early manhood. One hung himself
in the garage; his sister found him.
The other waited till the family left
for a reunion he'd refused to attend,
arranged himself in an armchair,
and slit his wrists. It was a hot week,
and the smell from the apartment
alerted the neighbors.

Worse than the dread were the discoveries.
The nightmares have never gone away.

What do you want from me?
You were the one who left—
Why won't you let me go?
Whatever I did that was wrong,
I'm still paying for it.

DAVID LOHREY

Licorice Waters

The horror of being on black water. That was it.
  You sit in a boat that's not moving, in the shade
  with the jungle behind you. Say what you will,
  the Amazon is not the Mississippi. It may be long
  and merry, but it is not muddy or murky. It's sleek
  and shiny like a child's candy. The Amazon,
  the color of licorice, glistens. It laps at the cashew
  groves in a different hue, something like whiskey.

I wait. I watch. I look. I listen, with the piranha
  churning. The water is not green or brown like mud.
  The river is black as a samurai's topknot. I feel like a soldier.
  The water is torn by passing boats. The noise scares some,
  but not the piranha.
  They're not so easily fooled. They take the bait but
  bite with care. They eat around the hook.
  And I wait in the black water all day or for years,
  hoping for a break.

Finally, at midday, I paddle away, down to a less vibrant
  part of the river and drop my line. I am left to fish without bait.
  Here I wait, drifting, above the blackness. I watch for the toucan.
  I whistle. I wave and the people wave back. "I have friends."
  I learn to survive. The tiny flesh-eaters feast without anger.
  Their desperation is instinctive. Their motivation, survival.

Hemingway always wanted to get things right. He had

an obsession with accurate observation. The imagination

creates distractions. He chose despair over fantasy; as I did,

once. Even he, a man of bluer waters, would feel alone here;

in the darkness, the clouds gather, reflecting the still water.

Into this ravenous mass I lower my hook baited now

with bits of ham sandwich.

Like a teacher's stick of chalk, my line descends into the

darkness, black as ink. The water's color is sinister. To fall

in would be like diving into an open grave, I imagine, not

drowning but disappearing. The river water runs into

the jungle like mascara. I wait as a hitchhiker on a country

road. If lucky, a toucan will fly by, delivering color, a small flash

of rainbow; otherwise, it promises to be a dark day.

I float on water that is still. The sun doesn't have much longer.

There are no stars in the sky, no moon in the river. I can imagine

the frenzy below. I can feel the anticipation. It reminds me of

visiting Rothko's Chapel, its bleak walls in black, I sat within

in silence surrounded by city traffic. I haven't had a bite.

I should have made a move. Even the toucan has stopped flying.

Once caught, the little monsters are less menacing, their jaws

slacken; their bodies, scaled and gutted,

can be grilled on an open fire.

KATIE AFSHAR

The Escapists

My friend with the glossy
   curls and grey eyes once
   tried to save a relationship
   by moving to the big island
   with her lover. The locals
    ejected the organic coffee
   cart they'd built from scratch
   and bullied the couple down
   a dirt road. She found work
   as a bar-girl, chatted up
   customers, sipped between
   smiles, leaving sticky lip
   prints on the glass tumblers.

Of course she fell in love with
   another man—an old Hawaiian
   who called her princess, like his
   granddaughter. The two
   competed for his attention while
   the living room bustled in pit
   bulls and paper plates soaked
   with barbeque.

Back on this mainland when it was all
   over, she told me her favorite part was
   the clouds that hung out with the
   island like best friends. I could feel
   humid air when she said it, the frothy

shoreline, palm fronds wavering over
volcanic sand—I thought how I'd
grown skittish that year, always
checking my refection in the rear view
as I drove, watching my inbox and the
blunt winter sky for signs of change.

So when I waited for the
mechanic to repair the clutch on
my old Toyota and spotted that
skinny kid in the mounted TV
screen who jumped the chain link
at the San Jose airport
and stowed away in the wheel
well of a Hawaiian Islands
passenger plane I couldn't help
think as he stumbled over the
Maui tarmac stunned from oxygen
deprivation and below zero chill,
that I am seduced also by the
pretty lady painted on the fuselage
a plumeria behind her ear even up
against California's edge I want
the next edge a line of green
bumps way out in the Pacific
because what if I didn't leave
enough distance behind me?

DON CELLINI

Naming the Birds

Purple-black iridescent feathers,
the birds travel in noisy groups.
Listen to their sound:
tcha-tcha-tcha-tcha-tcha.
On the south side of the
Río Bravo del Norte,
they are called *urracas.*

In the spring, the dead appear
like wild flowers in the desert,
dehydration and heatstroke,
several hundred each year.
Those who die in the river swell up,
turn green, smell putrid.
Few carry identification.
Some border-town cemeteries
are filled with unknowns,
their plots identified
only with date and location.

When they cross the river and
pause on the barbed wire or roost
in the old mesquites, listen.
They make a sound like:
tchaayk tchaayk tchaayk.
On the north side of the Rio Grande,
they are called jackdaws.

We have named the birds,
we have named the river,
but we bury the dead
without a name. Listen.

SAMANTHA MALAY

Yelm

You can stand in the doorway to look at the night
  and pray against a family fate
  of muddy yards and porch pianos

  seek comfort in upkeep
  wasps beyond the ladder's reach
  a sliver of soap on the edge of the sink
  the glitter of glass shards beneath a broom

  picture yourself covered in leaves
  pockets emptied of matchbooks and coins
  limbs no longer hinged for gait
  far from the grasp of hasty plans

SAMANTHA MALAY

House 4

ANTHONY THOMAS LOMBARDI

island coordinates where the rumpus will commence or Maurice Sendak dictates my adult relationships

We've reached a time of year where the sun's glow doesn't

  bounce off the buildings in SoHo

        as much as slide off so no

  you're not permitted to blink

  yet.

  tank tops co-mingle with puffer vests & fine-knit caps & we choose

  which way to walk whether it's into direct light

      or into the Met or i guess i should

      mention a museum that doesn't breathe.

  what a marvelous way to

  live!

  except the most ardent poems or the most trivial matters — i

  saw someone wearing shorts & sandals & the temperature

  hasn't even broken 50 yet doesn't that make you mad? — don't

  occur without your outline against a city that hasn't reached its

  dog-eared potential.

  stepping off at Fulton Street the train platform attempts to

  devour every transplant (alive)

but isn't the light after the cave supposed to
temporarily blind us or at least sting our
eyes?
instead the aroma of coffee rousing Manhattan jostles me
like a stack of books & i'm eating my own tongue

since there aren't any AH-HA moments that stick to the
sidewalks in this weather — they just spin on their
heels with a sigh & find
shelter in
misspellings.

what i'm trying to say is wouldn't you remember being
woken up mid-dream? emerging from a sea of hiccups
& your clavicles become a runway for my
fingertips to find flight.

i can be underwhelmed or overwhelmed but have i ever just
been whelmed? the closest i've been to rhapsody is when i
tripped on a thunderstorm. i gasped so shrill i broke a string.

we're either over-worked or under-paid & the Japanese

had the foresight to coin a term for it — *Karoshi* — so
we can pinpoint exactly where we went wrong but: if grinding
my hands & wringing my teeth doesn't feel strenuous then
our ineludible quietus is just another day
away from your soft landing.

now cracks a tremulous heart. now swings a
useless stretch of highway — redirecting signs

& end-of-the-day work-songs to where they belong: a space-pod
with never-ceasing limbs & slabs of purple linen where we
don't exit as much as exist. where endings curl into pursed lips
& things to grasp. where every closed door is a metaphor for
your open legs.

please don't go — i'll eat
you up, i love you so.

ANTHONY THOMAS LOMBARDI

self-care as an
outtake from Melancholia

i don't look for trouble, i make it — all up here in the two cubic
feet of space i've managed to squeeze behind my eyes. your
lungs don't breathe, they burn,

& how long has it been since it didn't hurt to exercise a
natural bodily function?

i get into an argument with the
trees
        but they get passive
aggressive & refuse to acknowledge
the look of hostility
        i spent hours fogging up my bathroom
        mirror

        trying to
        perfect.

i haven't perfected anything since i learned to
cross the street without looking.
        miles & miles of dust mites swallow every
        sunset you've ever imagined.

it's cool — we'll just wait for the next one; it's hiding behind
jumpy extras in horror B-movies & film stuttering in a
projector that will only take a minute to correct itself & play
your most embarrassing bloopers
if you'll just please be patient for a
moment!

we have a lovely spread of half-baked
almost-ideas & feint love affairs that refuse to die
in the meantime.

i duck into every cafe on Carmine
Street to avoid people i think i know —
of course we can just ignore each other
but i have to relieve myself of the
　　　dirty looks the sidewalks are giving me somehow.

i try to mutter "i'm sorry i startled you" to the moon
that only exists when i cross off another calendar box

but there's something caught in my throat — it's an elegy
for my time spent pacing between your doorstep & the
Hudson River.

fuck it, the West Village don't know me like that —
you can't even remember my sober date. why
would i give you the time of day?

i'm tying a string of
lavender around the
doorknob & locking my
　mouth.

CLICK CLICK
CLACK

don't knock unless it's urgent.

JANET MCMILLAN RIVES

Sides

On one side rusted steel slats
covered with razor wire
curled snakelike, border patrol cars
parked randomly, cameras
with a three mile range.
All of this says stay in, stay out.
The same slats, other side
adorned with vibrant murals
convey an eager welcome.

In the fifties and sixties we'd go
to Nogales for lunch at Zulas
then wander to the Mexico side
to buy bakery goods, tinware,
vanilla, blue glass.
In college we'd cross to drink
zombies at La Caverna.
That searing afternoon in May
nineteen sixty-eight
we locked arms to celebrate
Border Beauty and Friendship Day
in Douglas/Agua Prieta.

Today we share a lunch of pork,
frijoles, lemonade,
buy bags of beans at Café Justo.
Together we walk the divide
side by side
our mixed language echoing
off a backdrop of orange paint
with gray swirls, butterflies,
two hands touching,
the art of harmony.

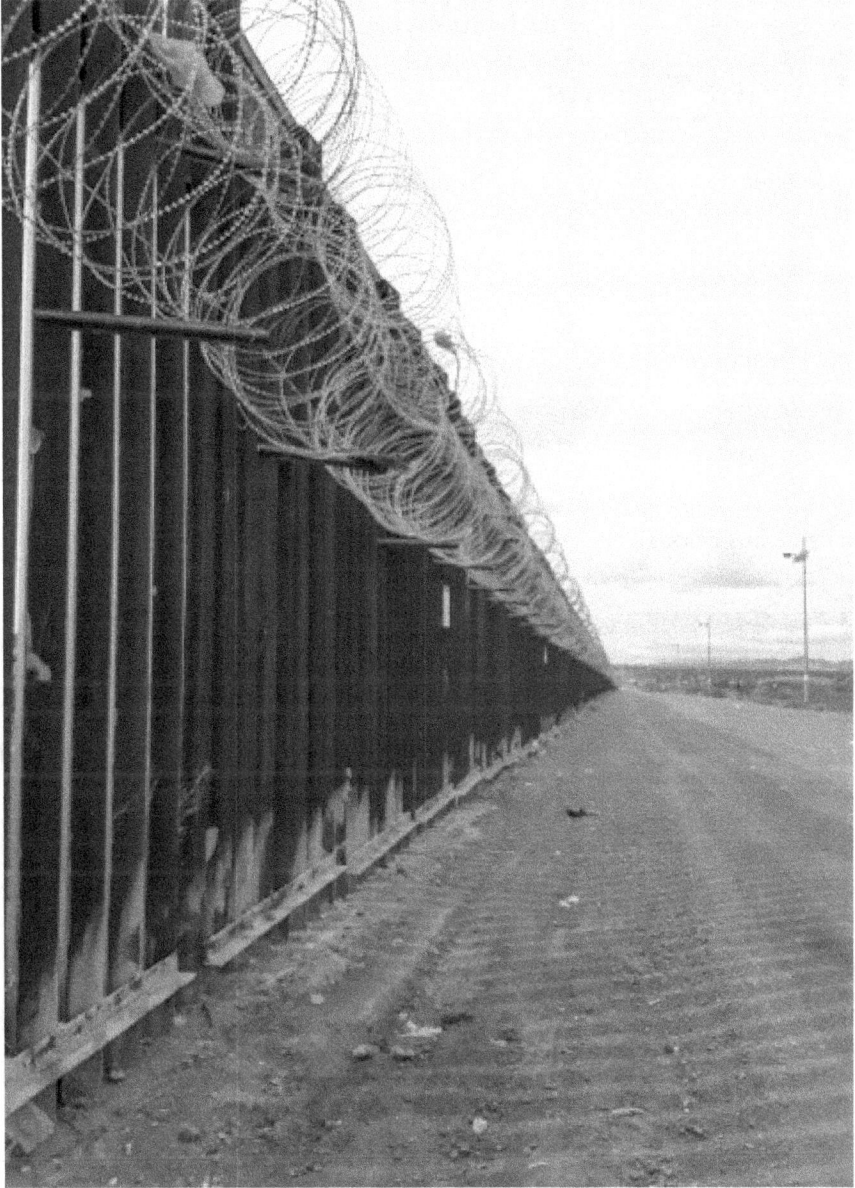

JANET MCMILLAN RIVES

Border Wall

JANET MCMILLAN RIVES

Border Words

Sinister	Sympathetic
Leery	Loving
Angry	Affectionate
Tense	Tender
Suspicious	Supportive

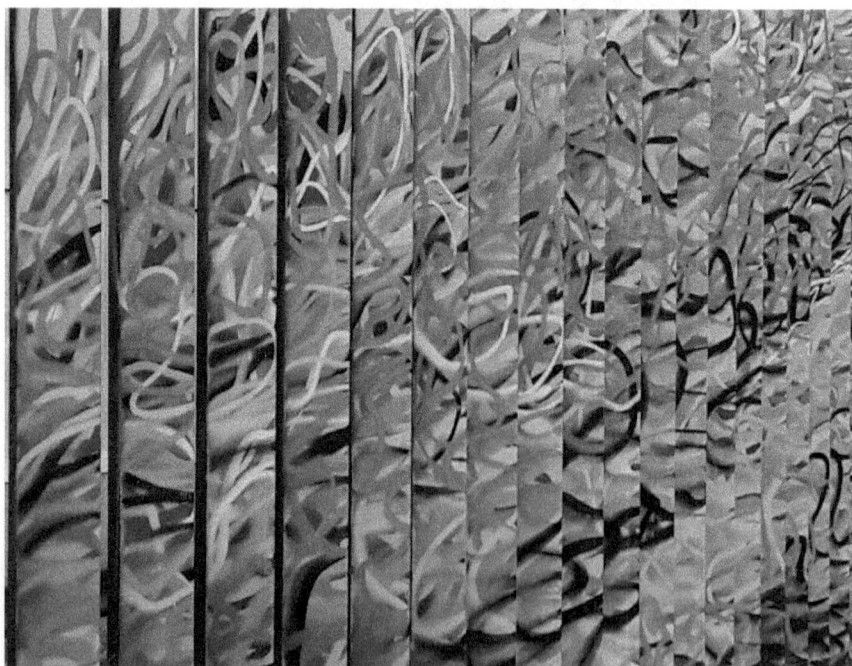

JANET MCMILLAN RIVES

Border Wall, Mexico Side

Procession

How much time does it take
　to cross the border
　if you are blue-eyed and blond?
　No time.　　And if you are not?

　You will sit in your car for hours
　waiting to come home
　after a day's work in Arizona.

　I see you there
　as I move with the others
　down Pan American Avenue
　our crosses held high.

　I imagine brothers　　sisters
　coming north　　no papers
　scaling the wall
　razor wire cutting　　hands　arms.

　If they make it to the other side
　thirst may kill them
　as they lie shivering
　on cold　　Sonoran sand.

　I lay down my cross

　Alicia Juanita Moreno
　18/6/1964 - 2/2/2003

　Presente.

JULIE A. SELLERS

Up Against the Wall

My words are up against the wall,
monochrome whispers
that slither along the outer rim
of the greater prismatic signified.
No alcanzan
estas alas luminosas
de tantos pensamientos,
su vuelo refrenado
por este vidrio opaco.
My words
mis palabras
up against the wall
contra el muro
two lonely tongues
dos lenguas solitarias.
But
juntas
I weave them
ensartando sílabas
like so many pearls,
una escalera de luz
that overcomes the limits,
que derrumba los muros,
words that fly on shimmery wings
en todos los colores de
my voice.

MARY SILWANCE

At the Border

Bueno. One more story, mija.
¿Ay, esa canción, otra vez?
Ándale or we'll be late for school.   mothers

Ok, another drink.
Sí, te acariciaré la espalda.
Mijo, it's past your bedtime.   may

¿Cómo dormiste?
No tengas miedo.
Mamá's right here, bebé.   never

¿Qué pasa, cariño?
Are you Hungry?
Lávate las manos, por favor.   get

Solo un ratito más.
Muy bien, chiquita.
I'm so proud of you.   to

¡Feliz Navidad!
¡Feliz cumpleaños!
Do you like your present, sweetie?   say

te amo
mi vida
mi alma   these
                         words
                again

como una llave

comme une clé

like a key

KEVIN CALLAHAN

Self Portrait

ARACELI ESPARZA

Sidewalks

Oh-oh, yo-yo
There are ghosts walking out here
Who used to work
Who fixed cars, cleaned houses, who cared for their children
This has never happened to me
But I see ghosts of my people walking
Out here on these streets.

Have you seen my sister, she's named after mi abuela
She never came home after school.
Her boyfriend says, he hasn't seen her in days.

We checked in the hospitals, but they said no one by that name
is here.
I see ghosts walking out on these streets
Who took them?

Last night, yo-yo, oh-oh
As I walked, I heard echo stories of these bodies who left
Everyone was watching on their phones and forgot to look at
the faces
Of who cleaned, who fixed, of who walked on these streets.
Who were part of our nation
Who had a function, a purpose
Where did they go?

Oh Oh, Yo Yo
I see ghosts walkin' on these streets.

POLLY ALICE

pensé

Little violet handkerchief folded on the ground,
    too shy to even show your face.
Je me souviens du bout courageux
    de ton menton, votre épaule nue.
You'll be brave again lift up your chin.

Et voici ton visage timide obscure un mercredi doré
    pincé au bord de l'hiver.
An gold Wednesday pinched at the edge of winter.
    Heart's-Ease, I know you've come to ease my heart
Je sais que tu es venu pour soulager mon cœur,

so dark from the strange angle
    of the distant white globe dans notre ciel.
Allons-y, let's wake from our icy sleep together.
    The sun, dear light, has come to wake us.
et rêve de nouvelles feuilles sur la terre noire.

Little violet, la pluie c'est comme tes yeaux
    La terre, comme ta barbe
the moss, plus verte que tout la monde
    Little violet, the rain it's like your eyes
The earth, like your beard

The moss, more green than anything
    Je, comme l'aire,
Je suis entre les arbres flottant derrière la brume
    I, like the air, I am between the trees
floating behind the mist.

Le printemps, elle chante. She sings and
Je suis content. I am happy. Je me lève.

HUASCAR MEDINA

Promesas

Ya mero llaneros
It won't always be this hard

Ya mero llaneros
They will embrace us

Ya mero llaneros
They will not fear us

Ya mero llaneros
They will accept us

Ya mero llaneros
They will respect us

Ya mero llaneros
They will not fight us

Ya mero llaneros
They will not attack us

Ya mero llaneros
They will not encage us

Ya mero llaneros
We will not be separated

Ya mero llaneros
They will not divide us

Ya mero llaneros
They will not send us back
to die

Ya mero llaneros
We will be welcomed

Ya mero llaneros
We will live in peace

Ya mero llaneros
They will see us as equals

Ya mero llaneros
We will be appreciated

Ya mero llaneros

They will call us family

Ya mero llaneros
They will love us

Ya mero llaneros
They will not hate us

Ya mero llaneros
It will all be over soon

Ya mero llaneros
We will forgive each other

JANET POWERS

Slipping Off the Verge

Today I woke up laughing
   with sea spray in my hair;
   as I cranked the winch
   the skipper smiled and said
   "You've done this before!"
   Ah, but the boat was smaller
   and the Chesapeake quiet,
   so these Pacific waves,
   exhilarating, challenge me.

   Sunlight streams, spume flies;
   we hurtle toward an island
   then come suddenly about,
   veering in opposite direction.
   Something to love about sailing:
   the excitement of pitting oneself
   against an unforgiving sea,

managing sails expertly,
sometimes slipping off
the verge of sheer control,
rail inches above the water,
till we shift to the other side
or let up on the mainsail.

If we intend to go the distance,
our tacking will be endless,
a journey marked by moments
of sudden shifts, tightened main,
precisely adjusted jib.
We will be fine tuning always,
testing the wind, seafarers
trusting each other to sail
just on the edge of the verge.

SAMANTHA MALAY
Night Bloom #3
(fragment)

TARA CARNES

Threshold

With a trembling hand
she turns the key in the lock
and opens the door

she couldn't have expected what she found
rhythms of life unfolding and unfurling
the next chapter of her story
yet to be lived, yet to be told

true she had never expected
to make it this far
had not made any plans

no preconceived notions of what was to come
no more disappointments of broken dreams

everything a gift
from this point further
she bravely
steps forward

KĒVIN CALLAHAN

50¢ Worth

Rummaging for a purpose long forgotten
  your hand emerges clasping a shining silver disk
  Is that a Ben Franklin?
  my curiosity always peaked by the unusual
  In the complete insouciance of innocence
  and carelessness of youth you proffer the collectible
  Intent on our evening parting I slip the treasure into my blues
  where it's memory will be lost, by you, to time
  Both memory and coin are with me yet
  a trivial gesture enduring decades and world wanderings
  How this small item (and that moment) endured
  remains a mystery that mirrors our journey of two
  Like an endowment your casual investment multiplied
  the value of a Franklin maturing twenty-fold
  A pittance that a Grand Canyon of treasure
  could not measure the yield on your 50¢ worth

POLLY ALICE

Excelsior

What is a poem? Is it something you write
and then just hope it's useful
for something?

asks my son standing on one
leg in the kitchen--
the kitchen where we make
pot roast sometimes on Sundays
and tamales in the summer
where ketchup flies
and paper lanterns hang
under the chandelier
where the dog-eared calendar hangs
crookedly and Grandma Twinkie
reigns as queen opening her mail
so carelessly, so carelessly
then slowly mixing her coffee
black and white every morning.

What is a poem, he asks the poet
on the anniversary of her liberation
on her anniversary to the day
six years ago when she
became the escape artist who
left with everything she could
carry.

Two mattresses, one old car
two children and her words
her words she stuffed inside
her shoes because her pockets
were full of ashes—Oh and the cat,
the cat came too.

                    II
A poem grows inside of you over time---
small as a strawberry seed so you wouldn't notice
it takes root, behind your teeth where words
form--- you must spit them out, so help you
God, or you will choke trying to swallow them.
Poems are what seeds are made from because
anything could form from them- and I mean
anything.

A poem is born when someone asks a woman to sew
her vision for a new democracy into fabric.
A poem tells you what stars may mean and
how a color might change a man and a
man might shape a nation.

A poem rises up when a people are lost though
lies and conquests, through the theft of
golden heads of corn, and the smothering
of wool blankets, the lies of interpreters

and the handfuls of seed beads stitched into
hides. A poem forms in empty spaces between threads
sewn in the shape of the hand of friendship
now behind glass in a dimly lit gallery.

A poem hides like a groundnut, secreted
underground inside its shell-- like when a man
loves something enough to wander through fields,
to go to school at night and work all day,
to put his science into words, to share his recipes
fold them into a book then carry it to family after family.
A poem blooms blue as chicory on the side of the road
and as open as the sky on June morning.

Poems spring from words scrawled on a guitar
carried by a man traveling road after dusty road
eating out of cans warmed in the fire
singing on the railroad tracks. Poetry
is handwritten lyrics on a matchbook—
a life that can never be unsung.

Poems are hard to kill. They coo like pigeons
they run like the tears of fathers into
their hands when they sit waiting for
their babies to return home.

Poems walk vigil in the
night when others go to sleep under blankets
of forgetfulness or folly. When a child on the border dies
because no one would give her a cup of
cold water, poems rise up to light her candle.

Poems rise up to call her lovely and place
a crown on her head.

Poems are like peas under the mattresses of
tyrants. They tuck in their toes and curl up into a ball
hard and insoluble so the power hungry cannot sleep
easy at night but toss endlessly in their many regrets.
They whisper into the ears of the greedy
the true love that might have been.

Poems guard the gates to happiness by hiding in locks
springing out metaphors into the palms of unsuspecting
hands with a jolt of electricity—I think,
they think this is funny.

Poems count the lost deep secrets as friends
and whisper their stories to refugees
hanging on by the memory of their mother's
voice singing a lullaby to the moon at night.

But when they are tired of holding the secret
truth of the universe silently in their bellies,
they sink down heavy as stones in quarries.
And if we lie down with them and dream, we
might hear the distant crystalline sound of our future,
an almost invisible hum like the sound the sun
makes before it rises when the world is still grey.

Should you meet a poem on the road, invite
it in and you will never, never be alone.

PAUL DRESMAN

Under The Dome

Under the dome, circling Polaris,
 we travel together through a lifetime,
 climbing steep trails to find lookouts,
 floating down one river after another,
 driving the streets, drowning in traffic,
 awakening to dreams clear as a bell.
 We come inside, out of the cold,
 when October winds clarify constellations,
 grateful for walls and feathered quilts,
 a longtime couple, growing old, slowly adrift,
 forgetful cartographers of the infinite.

MANO SOTELO

Contemplating Connections Between Fear, Hope and Faith

SAMANTHA MALAY

Night Bloom #23

The Very Edge
Poets
&
Artists

POETS FROM THE VERY EDGE

Katie Afshar is a pediatrician and writer from the San Francisco Bay Area who likes to garden at night and sleep during the day. She has been published in Rabbit Poetry Journal, Metonym, Cagibi, The Sun Magazine and in the anthology, Civil Liberties United: Diverse Voices from the San Francisco Bay Area.

Polly Alice studied poetry under Julia Kasdorf and many other narrative poets. Her art and poetry has been published internationally in Naugatuck River Review and arc24 and elsewhere, most recently in Rattle magazine. She is an adjunct writing professor and creative consultant; also the founder and managing editor of Flying Ketchup Press.

Omar Bárcena is currently a poet who tries to earn a salary by practicing architecture, or an Architect who tries to survive by attempting at poetry. His specialty at one of these things is hospital design and part of the job includes visiting and designing morgues. His other specialty is coping with the tearing that occurs when one has two motherlands, that more often than not, appear contrary to one another. Born along a desert border that divides two Californias, he was forced into bilingual education. Since the age of five, he played, grew, and was educated on both sides of an international border. Living two cultures, it was difficult to speak in either language without sacrificing beauty. Omar's communication was one of mostly verbal silence supplanted by the arts. Omar learned that poetry speaks like he does. Omar now hobbies with photography, reading, writing, pedestrianism, and swimming when he is not busy being an Architect a little further northwest from that border where he grew up.

Jill Bronfman is a professor, lawyer, non-profit worker, poet, and parent. In recent years, her work has been published in Mothers Always Write, Talking Writing, Coffin Bell Journal, Flock, Wanderlust Journal, Quiet Lightening, and a variety of books and periodicals. She has performed her work in Poets in the Parks and LitQuake.

Michelle Brooks has published two collections of poetry, Make Yourself Small (Backwaters Press), and Pretty in A Hard Way (Finishing Line Press), and a novella, Dead Girl, Live Boy (Storylandia Press). Her poetry collection, The Pretend Life, will be published by Atmosphere Press in November 2019. Her fiction, poetry, creative nonfiction, and photographs have appeared in the Iowa Review, Alaska Quarterly Review, Threepenny Review, Hotel Amerika, and elsewhere.

Kēvin Callahan calls himself the "Accidental Poet" as most of his poetry appears to him at odd times. His work is colored by his upbringing on a rural Iowa farm, his family, and extensive travel around the US, Canada, Mexico, Europe, and Africa. Kevin is an award-winning writer, painter, photographer, poet, and sculptor. His poems and art have been published in numerous anthologies. His collection of short stories run in his hometown newspaper.

Tara L. Carnes is a musician, composer, poet, teacher and spiritual director. She is a graduate of the University of North Texas (M.A.) and the Haden Institute's program in spiritual direction. Tara's poetry has appeared in Voices de la Luna, The Poetry Box, Illya's Honey, SageWoman Magazine, Cholla Needles Magazine, and Presence Journal. She lives in Houston, TX.

Don Cellini is a teacher, poet, translator, and photographer. The author of *Approximations/Aproximaciones and Inkblots*, collections of bilingual poems (March Street Press). His book of prose poems, translated into English, also the bilingual collection *Candidates for Sainthood and Other Sinners/Aprendices del santo,* and his translation *El silencio de las horas/The Silence of the Hours,* (Mayapple Press). A chapbook, *Stone Poems,* translated by Carmen Ávila, published in Mexico as *Piedra poemas.* He has published books of translations by Mexican poets: Elías Nandino, Roxana Elvridge-Thomas; Sergio Tellez-Pon; Rossy Lima; Jair Cortés; and the Venezuelan poet Amanda Reverón. He is a recipient of fellowships from the King Juan Carlos Foundation and the National Endowment for the Humanities, professor emeritus at Adrian College. He is the translation editor for The Ofi Press, CDMX. He and his husband of more than 30 years divide their time between Toledo and Savannah, Georgia. You can see more of his work at www.doncellini.com.

Paul Dresman was born in Los Angeles. He is a poet, a translator of poetry from Spanish, a co-editor of literary journals, including the bi-lingual helicóptero, and an essayist. He recently won the 2020 San Miguel de Allende Literary Conference poetry award.

Alan Dunnett works mainly for MA Screen at Drama Centre London, Central Saint Martins. His film-poem *'Interrogation'* (wrote/voiced) won Best Experimental Film at the Verona International Film Festival 2019. His poems have appeared in Skylight 47, The New European, Militant Thistles, Stand, Poetry News, The Rialto, The Recusant and London Grip; and anthologised in The Best New British and Irish Poets 2016 (Eyewear Publishing), New Poetry 6 (edited by Ted Hughes), The Methuen Book of Theatre Verse, The Robin Hood Book.

Following two pamphlets, a collection called *A Third Colour* was published by Culture Matters 2018. http://www.alandunnett.co.uk/.

Araceli Esparza is a Latinx Poeta, author and speaker with strong migrant farmer roots. She has her MFA in writing from Hamline University in St. Paul, Minnesota, and she's the Founder of Wisconsin Mujer and Latina Podcast Host of Midwest Mujeres. She's been published in many journals such as the Astri(x) journal. And was named one of the 2015 Women to Watch by Brava Magazine. Araceli Esparza's mission: to break the isolation of Latina women living in the Midwest. With close to ten years of being a cultural bridge for many local organizations, she has built a reputation of organizing engaging events that foster community and continue building change. Trained as a storyteller with a unique background in digital organizing, communications, and strategic planning, she cultivates authentic relationships with their audiences. You can hear Araceli Esparza tell more stories in her new project podcast: www.midwestmujeres.com.

Kristen Gallagher's most recent poetry collection is *We Are Here* (Truck Books, 2011). Since then: Florida, a chapbook from Well Greased Press, *Dossier on the Site of a Shooting,* a multi-platform digital work on GaussPDF, and Untitled (Rosewood Trip), text with screenshots, in Printed Web 3. Her essay *"Cooking a Book with Low Level Durational Energy; or, How to Read Tan Lin's Seven Controlled Vocabularies"* just came out in Reading the Difficulties from University of Alabama Press, and her essay "Teaching Freire and CUNY Open Admissions" was recently anthologized in Class and the College Classroom: Essays on Teaching. She is a professor of English at City University of New York–LaGuardia Community College in Queens, New York.

Malcolm Glass has published a dozen books of poetry and non-fiction. His poems, fiction, and articles have appeared in many journals, including "Poetry" (Chicago), "Prairie Schooner," "The Linking Ring," and "The Sewanee Review." His newest collection of poems, *"Mirrors, Myths, and Dreams"* was released by Finishing Line Press in 2018.

Jeffrey Hantover has written extensively on social issues, art, and culture for international publications, and his poetry has been published in several U.S. literary journals. He lived in Hong Kong for more than a decade and resides with his wife in New York City.

Donna Isaac is a teaching artist who helps organize community readings in the Twin Cities. Her published work includes a poetry book, Footfalls (Pocahontas Press), a paean to American folk music and her formative years in the Appalachians; two chapbooks, Tommy (Red Dragonfly Press); Holy

Comforter (Red Bird Chapbooks); and work in journals, e.g., Pine Mountain Sand & Gravel, The Penn Review, The Saint Paul Almanac, e.g. A new chapbook, *Persistence of Vision*, is forthcoming from Finishing Line Press, 2019. Find her at donnaisaacpoet.com.

Vicci Jacobs, a poet in the dusty heart of Southern Colorado, splits her time between parenting, teaching pottery, and earning her MA in English. Jacobs' work explores her time hitchhiking across the United States and her upbringing as a second-generation mime. Her poems and author interviews have been published in the Flint Hills Review, Tittynope Zine, and other fine publications.

A. Kaiser is a member of Sweet Action Poetry Collective and contributor to its four chapbooks. Her work can also be found or is forthcoming in Amsterdam Quarterly, Broken Plate, Conclave, Inscape, The Rumpus, WORDPEACE, and elsewhere. She is a 2019 finalist for the North American Review James Hearst Poetry Prize for her poem "Mary O. Davis;" "The Dogwood: A Journal of Poetry & Prose" Poetry Prize for multiple exposures; the "46th New Millennium" Writing Poetry Prize for "At the speed of light, squared, and the Eggtooth Editions Chapbook" Contest for Refract. A. Kaiser holds a doctorate in Intercultural Studies & Translation, with a dissertation on the first translations of Walt Whitman's "Leaves of Grass" into Catalan, French and Spanish, with a special emphasis on the Catalan translator, democrat and city-garden advocate urbanista, Cebrià Montoliu, on whose biography she is currently working.

David Lohrey's plays have been produced in Switzerland, Croatia, and Lithuania. In the US, his poems can be found at the The Drunken Llama, New Orleans Review, Nice Cage, and Panoplyzine. Internationally, his work appears in journals located in India, Ireland, Malawi, Hungary, and Singapore. His fiction can be seen at Dodging the Rain, Terror House Magazine, and Literally Stories. David's collection of poetry, *MACHIAVELLI'S BACKYARD*, is published by Sudden Denouement Publishers. He lives in Tokyo.

Anthony Thomas Lombardi is a poet / writer and former music journalist. His work has appeared or is forthcoming in Wildness, Third Coast, Gigantic Sequins, American Poetry Journal, Alegrarse Journal, Twyckenham Notes, Permafrost Magazine, Poetry City, and elsewhere. He currently serves as a poetry reader for the Adroit Journal, advocates for mental health and addiction awareness, and lives in Brooklyn, NY with his cat, Dilla.

Evamarie Lugo writes, "I am a Hispanic lesbian artist living and working in Tucson, Arizona. After many places in my childhood I found my home when I came to the University of Arizona, to study art, languages, literature, and philosophy. My work as a writer and as an artist honors everyday life. In my heart, these elegant simple everyday events become visual memories. What on the surface an essay, an article, poem, or painting is just paper or canvas, it becomes a study of space and color. To me, the sacred and the common mix and embrace in a dance that I would not dare separate. I feel that my work is a study of relationships hinting at the serenity of everyday life, like a table with flowers or the memory of a beautiful woman, long gone, reading poetry to her children. My work has been published in various magazines, anthologies, and newspapers. I make a living as a grant writer and translator."

Katharyn Howd Machan lives in a small city in central New York State resplendent with gorges and waterfalls and a long lake. Author of 39 published collections of poems—most recently *A Slow Bottle of Wine,* winner of the 2019 Jessie Bryce Niles Chapbook Competition—she teaches students creative writing in fairy-tale-based courses at Ithaca College.

Eric Machan Howd is an assistant professor of professional and technical writing in the Department of Writing at Ithaca College. His work has appeared in many journals and anthologies, such as: River City, Nimrod, The Healing Muse, and Yankee Magazine. His poem, Mycology, was the 2018 winner of the Switchback Poetry Contest and in 2019 he was invited as a guest poet/lecturer for a conference on American/Slovene poetics in Ljubljana, Slovenia. He recently completed a Masters of Fine Arts in Creative Writing (Poetry) at the Vermont College of Fine Arts. He lives, loves, and writes poetry with his glorious spouse, Katharyn, in Ithaca, NY.

Samantha Malay was born in Berlin, Germany, and grew up in rural northeastern Washington State. She is a graduate of Seattle University's sociology program, a theatrical wardrobe technician by trade, and a mixed-media artist. Her poems have been published in The RavensPerch, Sheila-Na-Gig, Burningword, Sky Island, The Sea Letter, Alexandria Quarterly, Quiddity, Projector Magazine, Blood Tree Literature, Heirlock, Genre: Urban Arts, Wild Roof Journal, Rougarou, Shark Reef, and Soliloquies Anthology, and will soon appear in The Closed Eye Open. Her published poetry can be found at https://thistleandhasp.wordpress.com.

Janet McMillan Rives grew up in Connecticut and Arizona. She retired as professor of economics from the University of Northern Iowa. Her poems have appeared in Lyrical Iowa, Ekphrastic Review, Sandcutters, The Blue Guitar, The Avocet, Fine Lines and The Raw Art Review as well as the anthologies Women Facing West, Voices from the Plains, and Desert Tracks: Poems from the Sonoran Desert. Her chapbook, *Into This Sea of Green: Poems from the Prairie,* is forthcoming fall 2020.

Huascar Medina is the seventh Poet Laureate of Kansas, 2019-2021. Huascar is a poet, writer, and performer who lives artfully in Topeka. He currently works as a freelance copywriter and as the Literary Editor for seveneightfive magazine publishing stories that spotlight literary and artistic events in Northeast Kansas. His poems can be found in his collection How to Hang the Moon published by Spartan Press. He is the winner of ARTSConnect's 2018 Arty Award for Literary Art. His forthcoming book *Un Mango Grows in Kansas* will be released in 2019. As Poet Laureate of Kansas, Huascar promotes the humanities as a public resource for all Kansans through public readings, presentations, and discussions about poetry in communities across the state.

Cécile Oumhani is a poet and a novelist. Among her books of poems: *Passeurs de rives* (2015) and *Mémoires inconnues* (2019), nominated for the Prix Mallarmé. Among her novels: *L'atelier des Strésor* (2012), Special Mention of the Franco-Indian Gitanjali Prize (2012), and Tunisian Yankee (2016), winner of the Maghreb ADELF Prize, nominated for the Joseph Kessel Prize. She was awarded the 2014 Virgil Prize for her work as a whole. Her books have been translated in several languages. A German translation of Tunisian Yankee was published in October 2018. She is on the editorial board of Siècle 21 and has been guest editor for Words Without Borders in the USA and Caesurae in India. She collaborates with Apulée. One of her prose poems written in English was published in Volume 4 of Poems for the Millennium, (The University of California Press, 2013). Other poems written in English have been published in magazines such as The Statesman in India. She participates in readings and literary festivals in France and abroad, like the 2017 International Poetry Festival in Trois-Rivières in Quebec. She is a member of the Francophone Women Writers' Parliament.

Eloísa Pérez-Lozano writes poems and essays about Mexican-American identity, motherhood, and women's issues. She graduated from Iowa State University with a B.S. in psychology and an M.S. in journalism and mass communications. A 2016 Sundress Publications Best of the Net nominee, her work has been featured in The Texas Observer, Houston Chronicle, and Poets Reading the News, among others. She lives with her family in Houston, Texas.

I am NOBODY the Poet, an anonymous poet located in San Marcos, Texas. My work has been previously published in Sybil Journal, albeit not under a moniker.

Janet M. Powers, Professor Emerita at Gettysburg College, taught for forty-nine years in the fields of South Asian literature and civilization, women's studies and peace studies. She has published poetry in many small journals, including Azure, Earth's Daughters and The Gyroscope Review. This old lady still writes poetry and stands on street corners with signs—trying to change this sorry world of ours. I do not have an author page, alas.

Bruce Pratt is an award-winning short story writer, poet, and playwright. He is the author of the novel *The Serpents of Blissfull* from Mountain State Press, the poetry collection Boreal from Antrim House Books, The Trash Detail: Stories from New Rivers Press, and the poetry chapbook *Forms and Shades* from Clare Songbirds Publishing. His fiction, poetry, drama, and essays have appeared in more than forty magazines, reviews, and journals across the United States, and in Canada, Ireland, and Wales. He is the editor of American Fiction and an adjunct instructor of Creative Writing and Literature at the University of Maine, he also teaches in The Honors College and serves as faculty liaison to the Women's Ice Hockey team. Pratt edits the annual anthology American Fiction and is the past director of The Northern Writes New Play Festival. A graduate of Franklin and Marshall College, he also holds an MA in English Literature from Maine and an MFA from the University of Southern Maine's Stonecoast Program. He lives in Swanville Maine with his wife, Janet. His website, www.bepratt.com.

Julie A. Sellers is an Associate Professor of Spanish at Benedictine College in Atchison, Kansas, and she is also a Federally Certified Court Interpreter (English/Spanish). A native of Kansas, Julie has travelled extensively in Latin America and Spain. She has twice been the overall prose winner of the Kansas Voices Contest (2017, 2019). She has published creative works in Wanderlust, The Write Launch, Kansas Time + Place, and Heartland!, among others. Julie's third academic book, The Modern Bachateros: 27 Interviews (McFarland, 2017), received the Kansas Authors Club 2018, It Looks Like A Million Book Award.

Mary Silwance lives in Kansas City. A mother, environmental activist, educator, farmhand, and poet, she has served as poetry co-editor for *Kansas City Voices* and is member of the Kansas City Writers Group. Her work has appeared in Konza Journal, *Descansos, Heartland: Poems of Love, Resistance, and Solidarity, Sequestrum, Well Versed, Rock Springs Review,* and on her blog, http://tonicwild.blogspot. com/. Her poems have won first place in Well Versed and Rock Springs Review.

Anne Whitehouse is the author of six poetry collections, most recently *Meteor Shower* (Dos Madres Press, 2016). She has also written a novel, *Fall Love,* which is now available in Spanish translation as *Amigos y amantes* by Compton Press. Recent honors include 2018 Prize Americana for Prose, 2017 Adelaide Literary Award in Fiction, 2016 Songs of Eretz Poetry Prize, 2016 Common Good Books' Poems of Gratitude Contest, 2016 *RhymeOn!* The 2016 F. Scott. and Zelda Fitzgerald Museum Poetry Prize. She lives in New York City. www. annewhitehouse.com

J. Weintraub has published fiction, essays, translations, and poetry in all sorts of literary reviews and periodicals, from The Massachusetts Review to New Criterion, from Prairie Schooner to the Chicago Reader. Many of his pieces have been anthologized, and he has received awards for fiction and creative nonfiction from the Illinois Arts Council, the Barrington Arts Council, and Holy Names University, among others. He has been an Around-the-Coyote poet, a StoneSong poet, and as a member of the Dramatists Guild, he has had radio plays, staged readings, and one-act plays produced throughout the USA and in Australia, New Zealand, and India. As a translator he has introduced the Italian horror writer, Nicola Lombardi, to the English-speaking world, and in 2018 his annotated translation of Eugène Briffault's *Paris à table: 1846* was published by Oxford University Press. Website: https://jweintraub.weebly.com/.

Megan Wildhood is a creative writer and social services worker in Seattle, WA, whose work includes a poetry chapbook *Long Division* (Finishing Line Press, 2017), which is about sororal estrangement; essays, fiction, poetry and nonfiction that have appeared, among other publications, in *The Atlantic, The Sun, and Yes!* Magazine and a novel in progress. She's a guest writer for the blog *Women in Theology.* She wants to connect with readers, activists and weary humans around issues of mental health, challenging dysfunctional systems conflict and defiant hope in these tattered days. You can learn more at meganwildhood.com.

Guinotte Wise has been a creative director in advertising most of his working life. In his youth he put forth effort as a bull rider, ironworker, laborer, welder, funeral home pickup person, bartender, truckdriver, postal worker, ice house worker, paving field engineer. Wise is a sculptor, sometimes in welded steel, sometimes in words. Educated at Westminster College, University of Arkansas and Kansas City Art Institute. Tweet him @noirbut or FB @ RenoPeteStCyr. Guinotte Wise writes and welds steel sculpture on a farm in Resume Speed, Kansas. His short story collection *Night Train, Cold Beer* won publication by a university press and enough money to fix the soffits. Six more books since, a five-time Pushcart nominee, his fiction and poetry have been published in numerous literary journals including Atticus, The MacGuffin, Southern Humanities Review, Rattle and The American Journal of Poetry. His wife has an honest job in the city and drives 100 miles a day to keep it. Find more of his work is at http://www.wisesculpture.com.

SAMANTHA MALAY

Night Bloom #3
(fragment)

ABOUT THE COVER ARTIST

Samantha Malay, Artist and Poet was born in Berlin, Germany and grew up in rural northeastern Washington State. She is a graduate of Seattle University's sociology program, a theatrical wardrobe technician by trade, and a poet. Inspired by the plant kingdom and her collection of vintage textiles, she works with reclaimed fabric, travel ephemera and beeswax to create new textures and patterns. Her mixed-media images have been published in The Grief Diaries, Cahoodaloodaling, Phoebe: A Journal of Literature and Art, Temenos, Chaleur Magazine, Apeiron Review and Inverted Syntax.

The Night Bloom pieces belong to a series of collages made from snapshots of old movies, reclaimed fabric and beeswax. They are glimpses of a dark house on a late summer evening, crickets heard through a screen door, a clothesline fluttering in an empty back yard. Before moving to a remote homestead, my family lived itinerantly. We gleaned abandoned furniture on twilight alley walks, found clothes and dishes at Salvation Army, and slept under the stars in campgrounds and fields. I use salvaged pillowcases and bedsheets in my mixed-media work because their floral designs and threadbare texture signify both the idea of home and the things we leave behind. Suspended in beeswax, an ancient archival material, my images are honey-scented mementos that never decay. I named my collage series after the night-blooming phenomena of plants like jasmine, cereus and moonflower, the most beautiful and fragrant in low light.

Night Bloom #3' analogue collage by Samantha Malay;
antique bed linens, snapshot of old movie, beeswax

'Night Bloom #13' analogue collage by Samantha Malay;
antique bed linens, snapshot of old movie, beeswax

'Night Bloom #23' analogue collage by Samantha Malay;
antique bed linens, snapshot of old movie, beeswax

'House #4' photo by Samantha Malay; Highway 99, Seattle, Washington

'House #6' photo by Samantha Malay; Highway 99, Seattle, Washington

'Parking Lot #4' photo by Samantha Malay; Highway 99, Seattle, Washington

ABOUT THE FEATURED ARTIST

Mano Sotelo: BFA Otis Art Institute Parsons School of Design, MFA in Painting from Academy of Art University. Mano's work has been exhibited at the Coutts Museum of Art, Alexandria Museum of Art, Tampa Museum of Art, Coos Art Museum, Tucson Museum of Art, University of Arizona Museum of Art, Arizona-Sonora Desert Museum, Tucson Desert Art Museum, Phoenix Art Museum, local and national juried and invitational shows, and a variety of Tucson galleries. Mano's work has also been highlighted in competitions hosted by The Artist's Magazine and International Artist Magazine. His work can be seen at www.sotelostudio.com or Instagram: @manosoteloartist.

"My overall artistic practice can be divided into two general categories: observational, and the contemplation of beliefs and values. My main objectives in painting are: observation, contemplation, meditation and prayer."

Contemplating Connections Between Fear, Hope and Faith,
oil on panel, 8" x 10"

Accountability, Polarity and Separation, oil on panel, 36" x 36"

Overcome the World, Savior 6, Oil on panel, 30" x 40"

ABOUT THE EDITORS

POLLY ALICE MCCANN poet, artist, dreamer says that POETRY saved her life. She began writing professionally after a cold January trip to the desert sleeping on the hard desert floor with only a book for a pillow. She studied poetry under Julia Kasdorf and many other narrative poets including her creative thesis on poetry and short fiction under Jacqueline Briggs Martin, and her critical thesis in Biography and the subconscious writing process with Claire Rudolph Murphy, for her M.A. in writing at Hamline University in St. Paul.

Polly's lyrical narrative poetry, explore her family's Midwest oral folk tradition, the role of women, and small meditative studies on the clash of faith, nature, and everyday items— for more work by this author. Polly has been published in Naugatuck River Review and arc24, and elewhere. She is the owner of New Thing Art Studio in downtown Overland Park, KS.

Polly Alice says her greatest poetry moments so far:
When the first poetry collection I edited that wasn't my own became an award-winning performance, I really felt like editing poetry and sharing poetry with the world was one of the most rewarding things I've ever done.

Find her poetry books online: *Kinlight, Tea with Alice* and 2020 release *Puss 'N Böotes: Dark Poems*. She is the founder and managing editor of Flying Ketchup Press. As a poetry editor since 2018, she's seen her poets gain awards and new audiences for their work.

ARACELI ESPARZA is a Latinx Poeta, author and speaker with strong migrant farmer roots. She has her MFA in writing from Hamline University in St. Paul, Minnesota, and she's the Founder of Wisconsin Mujer and Latina Podcast Host of Midwest Mujeres. She's been published in many journals such as the Astri(x) journal. And was named one of the 2015 Women to Watch by Brava Magazine. Araceli Esparza's mission: to break the isolation of Latina women living in the Midwest. With close to ten years of being a cultural bridge for many local organizations, she has built a reputation of organizing engaging events that foster community and continue building change. Trained as a storyteller with a unique background in digital organizing, communications, and strategic planning, she cultivates authentic relationships with their audiences. You can hear Araceli Esparza tell more stories in her new project podcast:
www.midwestmujeres.com.

DESIGN

The Art Director on this book was Kēvin Callahan. Kēvin is the author of many short stories, poems and a novel. His book *ROAD MAP- Poems, Paintings & Stuff* is available through Flying Ketchup Press in print and Ebook.

Callahan earned a BFA from Drake University with painting graduate studies at SFAI and SAIC–OxBow. He currently works and resides with his wife in Parkville, MO.

For more info contact the designer at kevin@bsfgadv.com

ABOUT THE TYPEFACE

The typeface chosen for this book is the family Gill Sans, lauded for its simplicity, readability, and real beauty. Our team went back and forth between the idea of "being on edge, speeding along the verge of escape" and the idea of the "glass house" a stillness and balance. What you have is our mix. You can imagine riding along the road stopping by each dwelling and those hitchhiking on the road. This is a trip. We stop to pick up each poet as we share together our stories along the way. Each voice unique and carried on the wind.

Kēvin also chose for the headings the ITC American Typewriter (Joel Kaden and Tony Stan, 1974), the most prolific modern example of a proportional typeface that emulates typewriter fonts was chosen by the designer to give the reader the impression of both speed and stasis and the rhythm of continuing on. Bebas Neue designed by Ryoichi Tsunekawa was chosen for its contemporary feel to bring us back to the present and our immediacy as artists calling out from the edge to cross boundaries and borders, to reach each other.

MORE POETRY COLLECTIONS BY FLYING KETCHUP PRESS

- *kNew: The Poetic Screenplay* by T.L. Sanders
- *kNew: The Chapbook* by T.L. Sanders
- *Sweetened Condensed:* Poetry & Photographs by Rebecca Grabill
- *Road Map: Poems Paintings & Stuff* by Kēvin Callahan
- *Blue City Poets: Kansas City* edited by Polly Alice McCann
- *Tea with Alice: Heirloom Poems* by Polly Alice McCann
- *Kinlight: Homegrown Poems* by Polly Alice McCann
- *Puss 'N Boötes: Dark Poems* by Polly Alice McCann
- *Night Forest: Poems* our 2020 winners coming 2021
- *Sprouts: Meditations from Artists & Poets* coming 2021

* Congrats to Hasna Salam our Poet in Residence 2020,
her collection coming 2021.

Flying Ketchup Press A Kansas City Publisher for the epic acceleration of great literature, poetry, children's books and fine arts materials. Our mission: to discover and develop new voices in poetry, drama, fiction and non-fiction with a special emphasis in new short stories. We are a publisher made by and for creatives with the spirit of the Heartland. Our dream is to salvage lost treasure troves of written and illustrated work- to create worlds of wonder and delight; to share stories. Maybe yours.

www.ingramcontent.com/pod-product-compliance
Lightning Source LLC
Chambersburg PA
CBHW071441090426
42737CB00011B/1740